OSPREY AIRCRAFT OF THE ACES • 10

# Hellcat Aces of World War 2

SERIES EDITOR: TONY HOLMES

OSPREY AIRCRAFT OF THE ACES • 10

# Hellcat Aces of World War 2

Barrett Tillman

OSPREY
AEROSPACE

**Front cover**
Ranking US Navy ace of the war, and premier Hellcat exponent, Cdr David McCampbell (along with his wingman) waged his own personal war on a formation of 80 'hostiles' on the morning of 24 October 1944 – the opening day of the Battle of Leyte Gulf. Already the Navy's leading ace, CAG McCampbell had been warned by his superiors that his loss in combat would be a serious blow to morale, and at 34 years of age he should let the younger charges in VF-15 take the fight to the Japanese. However, on this day all of *Essex*'s fighter pilots were needed to defend the task force, and McCampbell insisted that he was still a 'fighter pilot', so should launch too – approval for his participation in this sortie was hurriedly granted at flag bridge level!

Owing to the fact that McCampbell was not scheduled to fly, and that *Minsi III* was never flown by any one else, the fighter had been spotted in the hangar deck unprimed for combat. When word was received that the CAG was to launch, it was hurriedly brought up to the 'roof' and filled with as much fuel as time permitted – a full drop tank and partially full fuselage tanks. In this configuration he launched from *Essex* in near record time, leading the last seven Hellcats of 'Fighting 15' skyward to intercept an incoming raid of awesome proportions. Smoking a cigarette throughout the patrol, the CAG duly set about scything down the huge Japanese formation in F6F-5 *Minsi III* (BuNo 70143), and by the time he disengaged 90 minutes later, having exhausted both his fuel and ammunition, McCampbell had claimed nine fighters destroyed and a further two as probables – this specially-commissioned Iain Wyllie painting shows the first of five Zekes claimed by McCampbell diving away trailing smoke and flame. Realising that he had insufficient fuel to make *Essex*, CAG-15 diverted to USS *Langley*, and moments after completing a smooth recovery, his engine spluttered to a stop through fuel starvation

First published in Great Britain in 1996
by Osprey, an imprint of Reed Consumer Books Limited
Michelin House, 81 Fulham Road,
London SW3 6RB
and Auckland, Melbourne, Singapore and Toronto

ISBN 1 85532 596 9

Edited by Tony Holmes
Page design by TT Designs, T & S Truscott

Cover Artwork by Iain Wyllie
Aircraft Profiles and Scale Drawings by Mark Styling
Figure Artwork by Mike Chappell
Captions and Plates Commentary by Tony Holmes

Printed in Hong Kong

Acknowledgements
The editor would like to thank the various Hellcat pilots who corresponded with the profile artist in order to obtain the most accurate renditions of their aircraft ever to appear in print. Similarly, thank you to Stanley Orr for recounting his Fleet Air Arm exploits, and for providing photographs from his collection. On this latter note, acknowledgement also to *Aeroplane*, *Aerospace Publishing*, Philip Jarrett, Jerry Scutts, CWO4 Carl Snow of the *Tailhook* Association and Ray Sturtivant. Finally, thank you to Peter Mersky and Norman Polmar for their valued assistance.

EDITOR'S NOTE
To make this new series as authoritative as possible, the editor would be extremely interested in hearing from any individual who may have relevant photographs, documentation or first-hand experiences relating to the elite pilots, and their aircraft, of the various theatres of war. Any material used will be fully credited to its original source. Please write to Tony Holmes at 1 Bradbourne Road, Sevenoaks, Kent, TN13 3PZ, Great Britain.

# CONTENTS

# ACES MAKER

uring World War 2, some 1300 American fighter pilots were credited with destroying five or more enemy aircraft in aerial combat. Of these, 371 served in the US Navy and 124 in the Marine Corps. Thus, over one-third of all American fighter aces involved in the conflict wore naval aviation's beautiful wings of gold.

Unlike the Army Air Force, which flew eight primary fighter aircraft during the war (including the British Spitfire and Beaufighter), the two navalds during three – the Grumman F4F/FM Wildcat, F6F Hellcat and Chance Vought F4U Corsair. Consequently, Navy and Marine aces were consolidated more closely by aircraft type, and that is why the Hellcat became America's all-time champion 'ace maker' with 307 pilots credited with five or more kills in type. By comparison, North American's P-51 Mustang produced some 275 USAAF aces.

On the other hand, there were relatively heavy losses among F6F pilots. Throughout the war, combat-related pilot losses totalled some 450 aviators, including 20 Hellcat aces.

Although Grumman Aircraft Company produced the Wildcat fighter and Avenger torpedo aircraft, the Hellcat unquestionably became the Long Island firm's greatest contribution to the American victory. Built in large numbers (more than 12,000 airframes in three years), the F6F proved a near-perfect weapon for the war it had to fight. With a superb engine and no serious developmental problems, it was tough enough to withstand routine carrier operations. It was also reasonably fast, well armed, easy to fly and (perhaps more importantly) easy to maintain. In short, the Hellcat was a masterpiece of carrier-aircraft engineering and design. Small wonder that it became the most successful vehicle for a generation of American fighter aces.

**Whilst Wildcat pilots of the US Navy and Marine Corps were just managing to hold their own in the Pacific as the final months of 1942 slipped away, Grumman was hastily pushing its new fleet fighter through its test programme. This company shot shows second prototype XF6F-3 (BuNo 02982) on a test flight over upstate New York in late October 1942 (*Aerospace Publishing*)**

**As this photograph clearly shows, the first production aircraft completed at Bethpage by Grumman were finished at the factory in the Blue Grey (FS 36118) over Light Grey (FS 36440) scheme. This anonymous early-build F6F-3 is undergoing carrier trials aboard an equally unidentifiable carrier in 1943 (*Jerry Scutts*)**

## ORGANISATION

In 1943 the US Navy possessed 'fighting squadrons' or FitRons – the phrase 'fighter squadron' was a postwar development. When the F6F entered combat in the Central Pacific that August, each fighting squadron nominally had 36 F6F-3s aboard large (generally *Essex*-class) carriers (CVs) and about 24 to the much smaller *Independence*-class light carriers (CVLs). Land-based Navy fighter squadrons generally followed the organisational structure of the CV units.

The basic building block of a naval fighter squadron was the four-aircraft division, composed of two pairs, or sections. By 1943, naval aviators were skilled in use of mutual-support tactics based upon Lt Cdr John Thach's 'weave' pattern, proven in the Battle of Midway in June 1942. Developed to enable the Wildcat to survive against faster, more manoeuvrable opponents, the 'Thach Weave' was exploited by F6F squadrons whose aircraft was not only faster than the F4F, but climbed better as well.

Despite the success of the Hellcat in fighter-versus-fighter combat, the fleet defense mission assumed ever-greater importance as the Pacific war progressed. No other statistic better illustrates this point than the fact that, from mid-1943 to late 1944, CV F6F squadrons grew from 36 to 54 and finally to 73 aircraft. Successful *kamikaze* attacks, initiated in the Philippines campaign, placed a premium upon adequate fighter protection for the Fast Carrier Task Force.

The administrative requirements of dealing with six-dozen aircraft and 100 or more pilots finally led to the establishment of fighter-bomber (VBF) squadrons in early 1945. From a practical standpoint, the latter's operating methods remained identical, with both the VF and VBF units sharing maintenance chores and flying the same aircraft interchangeably. But making two squadrons out of one of course helped to simplify paperwork and enhanced operating efficiency. Complications only arose when carrier-based Corsair VBF squadrons flew alongside Hellcat FitRons, in which case mutual maintenance and logistics were simply not possible.

Owing to shipboard personnel limitations, Navy and Marine squadrons generally delegated collateral (i.e., non-flying) duties to most pilots. Under the three senior aviators – commanding officer, executive officer and flight (operations) officer – were relatively junior pilots in charge of gunnery, navigation, personnel, parachutes and emergency equipment, and assorted other areas. Usually a squadron contained only two non-flying officers – those responsible for engineering (primarily aircraft maintenance) and intelligence. Both were reservists, the fabled

The US Navy chose VF-9 at NAS Norfolk to be the premier fleet squadron to receive the F6F-3, the unit having only just returned to their Virginia air station following a combat cruise in the Atlantic aboard USS *Ranger* in F4F-4s – they had flown in support of the *Torch* landings on the North African coast. With its complement increased from 27 Wildcats to 36 Hellcats, VF-9 went aboard the equally new USS *Essex* on 13 March 1943 to carrier-qualify its pilots (*Jerry Scutts*)

Originator of the Commander Air Group's '00' (or 'double nuts' as the marking is often irreverently referred to by junior officers), recently-promoted Cdr 'Jimmy' Flatley, Jr, is seen climbing down from his personal F6F-3 after making the first ever landing aboard the second USS *Yorktown* on 6 May 1943 (*Jerry Scutts*)

VF-8 reformed on F6F-3s at NAS Norfolk in 1943, the squadron being commissioned on 1 June under the command of Lt Cdr William M Collins, Jr (who would eventually become the unit's ranking ace with nine kills). Seen on a training sortie over Virginia in late 1943, these F6Fs wear the newly-introduced tri-colour scheme and pre-war-style fuselage codes (*Philip Jarrett*)

Cdr Flatley keeps a watchful eye on a mixed formation of Hellcats and Avengers as they head for Marcus Island on 31 August 1943 – the date of the Hellcat's combat debut. No aircraft were encountered during the raids, and VF-5 had to wait until the 5 October strike on Wake Island to achieve its first kills. This 'Dash Three' was the second F6F assigned to the CAG (*Aerospace Publishing*)

'90-day wonders' being given specialised training as aviation volunteer specialists, or AV(S) officers. Even Annapolis men conceded that the Navy could not have won the war without them.

## CAMPAIGNS

Beginning in late August 1943, the Grumman Hellcat embarked on the first of a half-dozen major campaigns over the next two years. In those 24 months, the F6F would become the worst enemy of the naval and army air forces of Imperial Japan, downing (by official count) some 5200 enemy aircraft. Along the way, the angular Grumman produced more American fighter aces than any other aircraft in history – 307 in all. Additionally, F6Fs participated in the invasion of southern France in August 1944, adding a truly global dimension to the type's war-winning contribution.

Turning the clock back 12 months, by August 1943 the United States had in place the weapons and procedures which would yield naval victory over Japan. Foremost in the 'arsenal of democracy' was a new generation of carrier aircraft embarked in new ships – the versatile, long-lived *Essex* (CV-9) class and the much smaller, but equally fast, *Independence* (CVL-22) class of light carriers. Both types operated F6F-3 fighters.

First blood for the Hellcat was drawn by a member of a veteran squadron. On 1 September Lt(jg) Richards L Loesch of VF-6 caught a Kawanishi H6K near Howland Island. It was his only victory of the war, but began a Hellcat string of more than 5200 over the next two years. 'Fighting' Six splashed another 'Emily' west of Baker Island two days later, the first victim of future ace Thaddeus T Coleman, Jr.

The F6F's first two kills were scored by carrier pilots. But on 6 September, land-based squadrons in the Solomon Islands began logging a steady string of claims. The first fell to VF-33's Ens J A Warren, who downed a Zero near Margusiai Island. By month's end, Hellcats were credited with 35 shootdowns, of which 29 were scored by Solomons-based VFs -33, -38 and -40. Perhaps the greatest irony of the Hellcat's career was the fact that shore-based pilots out-scored their seagoing counterparts in the first month of combat.

On 14 September, 16 VF-33 Hellcats took off from Munda to escort an unusually large strike force comprising 72 Dauntlesses and Avengers attacking Ballale. Ten of the F6F pilots engaged Japanese aircraft, including Lt C K 'Ken' Hildebrandt who tacked onto a Zero trying to attack the withdrawing SBDs;

'I poured lead into him and he rolled over on his back smoking, at 200 ft. Tracers went by me then, so I pulled up sharply and collected

7.7 mm slugs through the cockpit enclosure. They went into my jungle pack and my back. The Zero turned away as I turned into (Ens Jack) Fruin who had another one following him. Firing from 100 yards, I continued through his pullout and roll. He went in when his port wing was shot off.

'Then I was jumped at 100 ft by a Zero. Using the hand lever to dump my flaps, I saw the Jap go by and pull up in a turn. I just held the trigger down until he blew up. Suddenly the sky was empty. Fruin was nowhere to be seen and I headed home.'

All F6Fs returned to Munda, reporting eight Zeros destroyed, though two Grummans were written off and their pilots wounded. Ken Hildebrandt added two more victories in December to become one of the earliest Hellcat aces.

The last kill of September was the first Japanese fighter claimed by a carrier-based Hellcat. On the 25th, Lt John Magda of *Saratoga's* VF-12 got a Zero over Barakoma, Bougainville. Magda, who had survived VF-8's Midway debacle, was eventually credited with four victories. In 1950 he led the *Blue Angels* aerobatic team (equipped with F9F Panthers) into action over Korea following the unit's mobilisation, and subsequent assignment to VF-191 aboard USS *Princeton*. Magda was killed in combat over Tanchon in March 1951.

During October 1943 the fast carriers began work in earnest. A major strike on Wake not only afforded the Navy with a long-awaited chance to avenge the Japanese seizure of the island in 1941, but to also introduce some significant new squadrons to combat.

Had the Japanese on Wake Island seen a roster of pilots assigned to fly on the 10 October strikes, they might have wondered if their German allies had changed sides. Flying with *Lexington's* VF-16 were

Often wrongly-captioned as showing a VF-35 F6F-3 from USS *Cabot*, this shot actually shows a VF-6 Hellcat going over the side of USS *Princeton* on 9 September 1943. The F6F suffered a sheared tailhook, which forced its pilot to 'throttle up' and attempt to take off before running out of deck. The Hellcat stalled and fell into the sea off the port side of the ship. The pilot survived his dunking and was picked up by the plane-guard destroyer (*Jerry Scutts*)

This flightline view of Hellcats at Munda (on New Georgia Island) taken in September 1943 shows *Navy* fighters of VF-33, -38 or -40, not *Marine Corps* F6Fs as has often appeared in print. All three units enjoyed success during their stay in the beleaguered Solomon Islands, claiming a shared total of 29 kills in their first month of operations (*US Navy*)

Munda was an important ex-Japanese Navy airfield taken by the Marines in mid-1943 and turned into a main staging base for new aircraft arriving in the Solomons. Again, these aircraft could be from any one of three Hellcat units operating in the area at the time this shot was taken in September 1943. Aircraft No 2 has the name *BATTLING Bobbie* emblazoned on its fuselage, and with the other more anonymous Hellcats, shares the jungle strip with a number of USMC F4U-1 Corsairs (*Tailhook*)

Another Solomons Hellcat 'flying in the face' of authority by carrying personalised nose art was VF-33's F6F-3 BuNo 25813, the mount of Lt C K 'Ken' Hildebrandt. *MY OWN JOAN II* was a deadly weapon of war when flown by the San Franciscan, who used it to down four Zekes and a 'Hamp' between 14 September and 24 December 1943. Both looking well-used following four months of solid combat, Hildebrandt and BuNo 25813 repose on Christmas Day 1943, less than 24 hours after they had both made 'ace'. VF-33 produced two other aces during its Solomons tour – Lt(jg)s Frank E Schneider with seven kills and James J Kinsella with five, although the latter's first two kills had been scored in February 1943 whilst flying F4F-4s with VF-72 (*'Ken' Hildebrandt via Mark Styling*)

aviators named Birkholm, Burckhalter, Frendberg and Schwarz. Cdr Paul Buie's squadron claimed six victories and Ed Owen's VF-5 off *Yorktown* bagged 17, while *Essex's* Lt Cdr Phil Torrey led VF-9 to four successes.

Lt Cdr E H 'Butch' O'Hare's VF-6, with VF-22, -24 and -25, flew from *Independence*-class carriers. O'Hare, who had won the Medal of Honour protecting the original *Lexington* from Japanese bombers, had not been in combat since February 1942 – this was his chance to make up for lost time (for further details see *Wildcat Aces of World War 2*, also by the author, published earlier in this series). Once the enemy formation had been sighted, he immediately led his four-fighter division into a mixed group of 'Zekes' and 'Bettys', destroying one of each while his second section got two more. One of the former fell to O'Hare's section leader, Lt(jg) Alexander Vraciu.

Always proud of having flown with 'Butch' O'Hare, Vraciu recounted his introduction to combat on the master's wing;

'I was "Butch's" section lead with Willy Callan as my wingman – "Butch" was leading with Hank Landry as his wingman. We high-sided a flight of three Zekes a couple of thousand feet below us. My radio was out completely, but I could sense what was happening. "Butch" burned the Zero on the left and I blew up the one on the right. It was my first aerial combat, and like an idiot, I was mesmerised by the Zeke. The lead Zero headed down and landed at Wake. I watched him land and burned the plane on the ground, followed by a "Betty" on the second pass.

'After our first pass, "Butch" and Hank ended up below some cloud cover, and according to "Butch" later in the ready room, ran into some "Bettys", and he got one of them.'

Including Vraciu, at least nine future aces counted their first kills among the 41 claimed at Wake that day.

This panoramic view of *Yorktown's* flightdeck shows Cdr Jim Flatley in his '00'-coded F6F-3 heading a line up of VF-5 Hellcats being readied for launch on 5 October 1943, the day that the US Navy returned to the skies over Wake Island after a long absence. The unit claimed 17 Zeros destroyed over Wake on this date

VF-16 'Fighting Airedales' F6F-3 is prepared aboard *Lexington* in November 1943. By the end of the year six pilots had made ace in the F6F, half of them from VF-16. The badge applied in decal form forward of the windscreen is in fact an Airedale, complete with pistol and flying helmet! (*Jerry Scutts*)

## FORTRESS RABAUL

During November two carrier strikes were launched against Rabaul, New Britain. On the 5th, Rear Adm F C Sherman's task group hastily organised a strike on Japanese warships reported in the area. The veteran *Saratoga* and the new light carrier *Princeton* put up almost 100 aircraft, almost half of which were Hellcats. 'Fighting 12' and '23' claimed 21 victories between them, with the TBFs and SBDs adding seven more. More importantly, six Japanese cruisers were damaged, thus preventing them interfering with the Allied landing at Empress Augusta Bay.

Six days later carrier- and land-based naval aviators claimed 137 victories – it was the first time that American fliers had ever claimed 100 shootdowns in a 24-hour period, and although Japanese losses were undoubtedly far less, it was still an awe-inspiring performance – and an ominous portent for the enemy of things to come.

Despite bad weather thwarting most of Sherman's pilots en route to the target, Rear Adm A E Montgomery's three carrier air groups were engaged almost non-stop throughout the day. A further indication of the intensity of the aerial combat is the fact that bomber and torpedo squadrons also claimed a dozen shootdowns.

Among the fighter squadrons, the most heavily engaged were *Essex's* VF-9, with 55 credited victories, and *Bunker Hill's* VF-18, with 38 claims. Elements of the

Despite their undisputed skill once engaged in aerial combat, none of the pilots featured in this, or any other, volume in the aces series could have achieved 'acedom' without the support of men like these back on the ground (or, as in this case, aboard ship). Fresh from keeping F6Fs airworthy during the Gilbert Islands campaign, plane captains from VF-18 pose for *Bunker Hill*'s photographer in December 1943 (*J D Billo via Mark Styling*)

VF-10 F4F veteran Lt 'Jim' Billo formates with his CAP leader astern of *Bunker Hill*'s Task Group in November 1943 whilst the rest of VF-18 'wages war' with Japanese forces over the Gilberts (*J D Billo via Mark Styling*)

latter carrier's original FitRon – VF-17 – paid a short visit as Lt Cdr Tom Blackburn led his F4U-1A Corsairs up from Ondonga, New Georgia, cycling aboard to rearm, refuel and enjoy a little hot food – the remaining half of the unit recovered aboard *Essex*. The 'Jolly Rogers' had added 18.5 kills to their scoreboard by day's end.

Top scorer among F6F pilots was VF-9's Lt Cdr H N Houck, with two 'Kate' torpedo-bombers and a 'Val' dive-bomber to his credit. At least 13 other Hellcat pilots claimed double kills.

Against fierce opposition the carrier aviators sank a destroyer and damaged four other warships, but the indications from the fighter battles were clear – Rabaul's days as a Japanese stronghold were numbered. Hardly had the smoke cleared at Rabaul when the fast carriers shifted targets eastward. Operation *Galvanic* – the occupation of the Gilbert Islands – was to also draw heavy aerial opposition.

Appropriately, 'Fighting Nine', the first squadron to receive Hellcats, also produced the first F6F ace. He was Lt(jg) Hamilton McWhorter, III, a 22-year-old Georgian who had first scored at Wake Island on 5 October. He added two more Zekes during the Rabaul strike and reached ace status during *Galvanic*. He splashed a 'Pete' floatplane off Tarawa Atoll on 18 November – the Navy's only victory that day – and his fifth victim, a Mitsubishi G4M 'Betty', followed 24 hours later.

Tarawa proved a brutal, bloody, fight for the Marines, but provided good hunting for the 'Airedales' of VF-16. On 23 November Cdr Buie and 11 other *Lexington* pilots were vectored into a formation of Zekes near Makin Island. Placed by the radar controller in 'a fighter pilot's dream position' 4000 ft above and 'upsun' of the 24 enemy aircraft, Buie and company chased down 17 'bandits' from 23,000 to 5000 ft. From that combat Ens E R Hanks emerged with five kills and a probable, thus becoming the first of 44 F6F pilots who would make 'ace in a day'.

Twenty-six hours later Buie led another batch of 'Airedales' into combat over almost the same spot, but this time the F6F pilots began the fight with a 2000-ft altitude deficit. Though one Hellcat went down in the Zekes' initial pass, VF-16 reversed the odds in an unusual combat which swerved upward and then down. When it was over, 'Lex's' Hellcats had splashed 12 more with Lt(jg) A L Frendberg claiming three Zekes to become the third F6F ace.

A by-product of *Galvanic* was the introduction of carrier-based nightfighters. Occasionally described in print as an impromptu effort, these 'bat teams' had in fact been organised and trained prior to their deployment. Their advocate and leader was 'Butch' O'Hare who, by November, was commanding *Enterprise's* Air Group Six. His assigned fighter squadron was temporarily VF-2, under Cdr W A Dean.

O'Hare's 'bat teams' were made up of individuals hand-picked for night interceptions, which they performed in addition to their squadron's usual daytime operational routine. The teams comprised two VF-2 F6F pilots directed by a VT-6 TBF equipped with radar. Operating in conjunction with shipboard fighter directors, the teams at least stood a chance of disrupting a nocturnal attack on a carrier force, if not actually destroying the raiders.

The acid test came on the night of 27 November following two fruitless Japanese efforts to locate the task group. O'Hare and Ens Warren Skon (himself a future 7-kill ace with VF-2) were teamed with Lt Cdr John Phillips, skipper of 'Torpedo Six'. Some 15 'Bettys' attacked the carriers, and Phillips' radar operator vectored him onto two bombers, which he shot down. He called for O'Hare's section to

rejoin and, in the process, it appears that a third Japanese bomber was attracted by the Avenger's navigation lights. The TBF gunner glimpsed a strange aircraft in the dark and fired a burst, apparently causing O'Hare to take evasive action. Whatever happened, 'Butch' O'Hare's Hellcat crashed into the water, along with its pilot. It was an irreplaceable loss.

Pre-invasion strikes against Kwajalein Atoll in December completed fast carrier operations for the year. Again VF-16 had the best of the shooting, claiming 18 of the 40 credited victories over Roi Island on the 4th. A number of

Shoulder to shoulder on 'Vultures' Row', a burgeoning number of the ship's company look on as the deck crew ready VF-9's Hellcats for yet another launch from *Essex* during Operation *Galvanic* (*Aerospace Publishing*)

these kills were claimed by 21-year-old Texan, Ens Edward G Wendorf, who downed a 'Betty' and three Zekes (although official naval records only credit him with two Zekes and a half-share in the 'Betty', with the remaining A6M being classed as a probable) – he also very nearly became a statistic himself, however, as he explains in the following report written specially for this volume;

'My BIG day had arrived. It was 4 December 1943! We went into Kwajalein as a group with three levels of cover to protect the dive- and torpedo-bombers – low-level cover at 7000 ft, mid-cover at 12,000 ft and high cover at 18,000 ft. I was flying "wing" on the division leader, Lt Jim "Alkie" Seybert, Jr, whose nickname must have stemmed from his earlier imbibing habits for I never saw him drink excessively in the time that I knew him!

'Jim's division was assigned as mid-cover. We arrived in the target area early in the morning at around 7 am, and proceeded to sweep the area for enemy "bogies". Seeing no opposition, we were directed to strafe Roi airfield, with parked aircraft (of which there were a few) and the hangar areas as our targets.

'"Alkie" put me in a right echelon, gave me the "break" signal, and peeled off to the left. I waited several seconds and commenced my attack. I kept "Alkie" in sight, but took a lateral spacing off to his right so that I could concentrate on my strafing targets and keep him in sight as well. I fired a few long bursts into a couple of aircraft on the hangar apron, then shifted my sights to an open hangar and fired a long burst into it. It was at about this time that I experienced several jolts caused by anti-aircraft shells bursting in close proximity. I "jinked and juked" (changed altitude and direction) several times to throw off their aim. We had agreed to rendezvous to the left of the field (over the water) at 5000 ft, but the AA was so intense that I had to break to the right.

'As I was commencing my recovery, I spotted a "Betty" bomber scooting low across the water. I don't know whether it had just taken off or was returning from another field. Anyway, I had to take off a lot of throttle as the speed from my dive was going to take me past him in a hurry. I swung out to the right and then back onto the "Betty". I fired a short burst of all six .50 cal guns which went over the top of him. I

**Catapult officer Lt Walter L Chewning, USNR, clambers onto the displaced belly tank of a VF-2 Hellcat to extricate its dazed pilot, Ens Byron 'By' M Johnson, from the flames. Both men survived this harrowing ordeal, played out aboard *Enterprise* during a recovery cycle on 10 November 1943 off the Gilberts, totally unscathed. Johnson later went on to score eight kills with VF-2 during the invasion of Iwo Jima in 1944 (*Aerospace Publishing*)**

**VF-16 pilots head out onto the deck in November 1943. Each had an allotted aircraft according to 6-kill ace Ralph Hanks (his was 'white 37' BuNo 08926), and pilots inspected 'their' F6F once a week. Despite this personal attention, he admits that due to deck spotting, pilots rarely flew their own F6Fs, and were not allowed to apply their names to airframes until late in the combat tour**

lowered my nose and sights and fired two longer bursts into the bomber. It started disintegrating and trailing heavy smoke, before commencing a slow diving turn to starboard and crashing into the sea (strangely, one of *Lexington*'s squadron intelligence officers credited a half-share in the demise of this aircraft to Lt(jg) Arnold H Burrough, an SBD-5 Dauntless pilot from VB-16 – this was his second "Betty" kill of the sortie, Ed.).

The stunted palm trees behind the taxying Hellcat show evidence of the bitter 'fire fight' that took place to secure the airstrip at Betio. VF-1 remained shore-based until 7 February 1944, claiming just a solitary Zeke kill (plus a probable) during its time on Tarawa – Japanese aerial opposition had been all but wiped out in the initial fighter sweeps of the Gilberts back in November (*Tailhook*)

'I then went full throttle and start a slow climbing turn to port, looking for Lt Seybert. As I climbed through about 7000 ft, I spotted a flight of four aircraft high in the sun, and since no enemy aircraft had been reported, I assumed them to be "friendly". We had been observing radio silence, and I hadn't heard any reports on the air. Little did I know that those "jolts" I had felt on my strafing run had been several actual hits in my fuselage of 40 mm type AA fire, and my radio had been knocked out of commission. I approached the flight of four from inside and beneath them, remaining unobserved. As I neared the formation, I was shocked to see that they all wore the red "meatball" of the Rising Sun, and were actually a flight of four Zeros!

'There was little I could do but slide out to the starboard side, line up the two outside aircraft and open fire. The outer Zero exploded almost immediately, and the second one began to burn and fell off to the right. Evidently, by this time the leader and the other wingman had spotted me and they broke in opposite directions. My only recourse was to follow one of them and I selected the leader. He turned steeply to port and I soon lost him. By this time the other wingman had pulled around onto my tail. I turned sharply to starboard and saw a couple of bursts of tracer go over my head. I dove to try and lose him but he stayed close on my tail.

'I executed a sharp pull up and as I neared the top and began to drain off my speed, for some unknown reason, I decided to pull it on through and complete a loop. As I was in the inverted position, I could see the Zero pulling through like mad and I realised that he was going to be in an excellent position to shoot me down on my recovery. It was at this time that I decided to push forward on the stick and fly inverted for a couple of seconds. The Zero was so intent on pulling inside me that I think the move surprised him and he lost sight of me, continuing his pullout instead.

'By delaying my pullout, and executing it a couple of seconds later, I found him just about in my sights on the recovery. I was slightly out of range at first and had to add throttle to close before firing. I don't think that he saw me until I opened fire, and by then it was too late as he soon began to burn, and then crashed into the sea.

Lt(jg) Ralph Hanks made history in 'his' F6F-3 BuNo 08926 on 23 November 1943 when he downed three 'Haps' and two Zeros (and possibly a third A6M) in minutes off Tarawa during his combat debut. This official shot of the young Californian was one of a number taken upon his return to *Lexington* (*Ralph Hanks via Mark Styling*)

'It had been an exciting several minutes, resulting in four victories – the "Betty" and three Zeros. There were several engagements going on so I decided to climb above the closest one, dive to get some speed advantage, and see if I could help pull an enemy aircraft off someone's tail.

'As I was climbing to get into the fray, I must admit that all of my attention was directed above me and not to my rear. All of a sudden I saw 7.7 mm machine gun and 20 mm cannon fire ripping off pieces of my wing covering, and tracer fire going past me. My first reaction was to turn my head and peek out from behind my armour-plated head-rest, but as I did so a 7.7 mm round came over my left shoulder, hit me in the the temple above my left eye and went through and out the front right-hand side of my canopy. It felt like someone had hit me on the side of the head with a 2 x 4 board. I was temporarily stunned and dazed, and I don't remember how long it took me to realise that I had been hit.

'My first thought was to "Get the hell out of there". We had been instructed that one of the best evasion manoeuvres was to dive to ter-minal velocity (I think the "red line" maximum speed allowed was around 400 to 425 kts) and make a sharp turn to the right. This I did and evidently it worked as the Zero pilot did not elect to stay with me, for which I was most thankful. As I pulled out from the high speed dive, I guess the "Gs" caused a draining of the blood for I noticed that the latter was spurting out and landing on my left hand, which was positioned on the throttle.

'I immediately placed my left hand on the artery leading to my wound and applied pressure. It seemed to stop most of the bleeding, but some was still running down my arm and onto my leg.

'For most of these raids a "Dumbo" (friendly submarine) was posi-tioned a few miles off the coast to rescue aviators who had been hit. In

One of the first west coast fighter units formed on the Hellcat, VF-1 had a most untypical introduction to combat during the Gilbert Islands campaign in November 1943 – it flew into action simultaneously from two separate vessels. Split between the escort carriers *Nassau* and *Barnes*, the unit performed mainly ground-attack sorties for the invading Marines, or CAPs for the task force. One of the first objectives of the Tarawa assault was the airstrip at Betio islet, for once it was captured VF-1 had orders to fly ashore to provide 24-hour close-air support for the Marines. After a bit-ter struggle, the runway was seized and the Hellcats flew in on 25 November – barely four days after the initial seaborne assault. This shot shows the F6F-3s arriving on this date, with a battered Zero pro-viding a sobering reminder of the airfield's former owners (*Aerospace Publishing*)

this case, I think the sub was off the northeast coast of Kwajalein, but the vessel stayed submerged until it was notified by someone that a flyer was down in the area. Since I was alone and had no radio due to AA damage, there was no way to communicate with the "Dumbo".

'I was still bleeding quite profusely, so it was decision time! Would I retain conciousness long enough to ditch in the area of the sub, get in my raft and take a chance on someone seeing me and notifying the sub of my position. Or, would I last long enough to stay in the air approximately 45 minutes – the length of time it would take to return to the ship and recover on board? I considered my options for a few moments and then decided on the latter.

'The compass heading for my return was around 045 degrees. As I attempted to take up this heading, I noticed that my RMI (remote indicating compass) was inoperative due to the AA hit again, and that the liquid compass was swinging through 30 to 40 degrees, thus rendering any reading extremely inaccurate. I decided to bisect a north/south and east/west runway heading on Roi, line up two clouds and fly in that direction. When I passed over one of the clouds I would quickly line up two more.

'The weather was mostly clear, with scattered clouds at about 3000 ft and four to five miles visibilty, so I flew most of the way above the clouds. At the expiration of 45 minutes, I decided to let down below the overcast and commence an "expanding square" search until I spotted the *Lexington*. I had completed two legs of the search when I spotted a carrier's wake, and I felt tremendously relieved.

'Unfortunately, I noticed the vessel's fantail boasted the numeral 10 – that of our sister-ship *Yorktown*. My wound had slowed to a trickle by now, but I was still losing blood, and was therefore anxious to recover on ANY carrier. As I flew by the island I waggled my wings to indicate that I had no radio, and also noticed that they had many aircraft turning up on deck ready to launch for another strike on Kwajalein. The visibility was still four to five miles and I looked all around but did not see the "Lex". I guess the people on the *Yorktown* realised my problem and used white material of some sort to make an arrow pointing in a southerly direction, adding the numerals 12 to indicate the miles to my carrier. I waggled my wings again indicating that I understood their message, and turned to that heading in search of the "Lex".

'After only several minutes of flight, I picked up the wake of the "Lex", and upon arrival noticed that the deck was clear and ready to accept aircraft. They immediately gave me a "Prep Charlie" in Morse Code with an Aldis lamp, indicating that it was OK to begin

With *Yorktown* recovering VF-5's Hellcats in the background, elements of VF-16 are launched from *Lexington* for the next strike on the Marshall Islands on 23 November 1943 – the latter squadron downed 17 aircraft on this date. Just above the Hellcat's centreline tank can be seen the silhouette of the escort carrier *Cowpens*, whose embarked flight of F6F-3s from VF-6 (12 aircraft in total) also participated in the day's activities
(*Aerospace Publishing*)

**Despite being weak through loss of blood from a head wound, Ens Ed 'Wendy' Wendorf still managed to get his F6F-3 (BuNo 66064) back aboard *Lexington* in one piece following combat over Kwajalein Atoll on the morning of 4 December 1943. He had claimed two Zeros and a 'Betty' destroyed on this sortie, before being 'clobbered' by an unseen enemy fighter (*Tailhook*)**

my approach, and subsequently a "Charlie" which meant it was okay to land. I turned downwind and began my approach. Much to my chagrin, I discovered that my tail hook rail had been shot away, and that I had no hydraulic pressure to lower my wheels or flaps. There was a compressed air bottle to blow down the wheels in an emergency, and since I definitely considered this such an occasion, I used it to lower my gear, and pressed on with my approach. The deck was clear, but as I approached the ramp I was given a wave-off by the LSO, who signalled to me as I flew past him that I needed to lower my tail hook and flaps. I waggled my wings again indicating that I understood, but that I was unable to do either!

'I continued upwind and began another approach. As I had opened my canopy and tried to use both hands to fly the plane, the wind blowing in my face, and the fact that I could no longer hold the pressure point on my temple, had caused the wound to bleed freely. The flowing blood was completely obstructing the vision in my left eye, and believe me it is difficult enough to land on a carrier deck with BOTH eyes functioning!

'As I neared the ramp on my second approach, I noticed there was a Hellcat crashed on deck in a "wheels up" condition. As I learned later, it was Lt Capowski, who had taken several 20 mm hits in the cockpit, and was severely wounded in the hand. They had brought him in on a "straight in" approach, and he was unable to lower his gear prior to landing.

'I was feeling OK except for the bleeding. I was not feeling faint or light-headed, and the wound above my eye was now feeling sort of numb – the caked blood was helping to stem some of the flow. Despite not feeling much pain, I did not necessarily relish the thought of circling for a while as the deck crew proceeded to clean up the crash, but I had no other choice.

'After approximately 15 minutes of circling, they again gave me the "Charlie" signal to land, and this time, realising that I had no tail hook or flaps, had rigged the barrier across the flight deck. This consisted of several strands of one-inch wire cabling to stop the aircraft on its run-out.

'I made my second approach and soon discovered that I could not see well enough to make the trap unless I held my left hand to my temple to stop the flow of blood. I made the approach in this configuration, flying the aircraft and making throttle adjustments, before eventually taking the "cut" with my right hand. I landed successfully and slowed my roll to almost a stop before I struck the barrier and nosed up. It had been an ordeal, and despite losing two quarts of blood, I had survived.'

After recovering from his wounds, Ed Wendorf completed his tour with VF-16, and went on to claim one more Zero and an unidentified bomber over Truk (29/4/44) and Guam (19/6/44) respectively. He saw out the war with VC-3 aboard the *Savo Island*, his official score remaining at 4.5 kills and two probables – all with VF-16.

Returning to the Kwajalein Atoll raids, Wendorf's CO, Paul Buie, who had already nurtured two aces among his junior officers, joined the ranks himself with three Zekes on the 4 December mission. He thereby finished the year as the top-scoring F6F pilot. The US Navy record, however, was still held by Lt(jg) Donald Runyon with nine kills, including eight as an *Enterprise* F4F pilot in 1942. At the end of 1943 he was back in combat, flying F6Fs with VF-18 from *Bunker Hill*.

### Land-Based Hellcat Squadrons in 1943

| | | |
|---|---|---|
| VF-33 | Solomons | 60 |
| VF-38 | Solomons | 7 |
| VF-40 | Solomons | 4 |

### Top Hellcat Squadrons of 1943

| | | |
|---|---|---|
| VF-9 | *Essex* | 65 |
| VF-33 | Solomons | 60 |
| VF-16 | *Lexington* | 55 |
| VF-18 | *Bunker Hill* | 50 |
| VF-5 | *Yorktown* | 21 |
| VF-12 | *Saratoga* | 15 |
| VF-6 | various CVs | 14.66 |
| VF-23 | *Princeton* | 14 |
| VF-24 | *Belleau Wood* | 7.50 |
| VF-38 | Solomons | 7 |

Total by 16 F6F squadrons – 323

### Top Hellcat Pilots in 1943

| | | | |
|---|---|---|---|
| Lt Cdr P D Buie | VF-16 | 7 | Total 9 |
| Lt(jg) A L Frendberg | VF-16 | 5 | Total 6 |
| Ens E R Hanks | VF-16 | 5 | all on 23/11/43 |
| Lt C K Hildebrandt | VF-33 | 5 | Total 5 |
| Lt(jg) H McWhorter, III | VF-9 | 5 | Total 12 |
| Lt(jg) A E Martin, Jr | VF-9 | 5 | Total 5 |
| Lt(jg) F M Fleming | VF-16 | 4.5 | Total 7.5 |
| Lt(jg) J Magda | VF-12 | 4 | Total 4 |
| Lt Cdr H Russell | VF-33 | 4 | Total 4 |
| Lt(jg) E C McGowan | VF-9 | 3.5 | Total 6.5 |
| Lt(jg) E A Valencia | VF-9 | 3.5 | Total 23 |

# THE YEAR OF DECISION

I n the Pacific as in Europe, 1944 was the year of decision in World War 2. First on the fast carrier agenda was the heavily defended Japanese naval base at Truk Atoll, in the Carolines, as Adm Raymond Spruance's Fifth Fleet planned a three-day surface and air bombardment in mid-February. Long aware of the mysterious, but fabled 'Gibraltar of the Pacific', many carrier aviators later admitted to suffering pre-raid nerves before the Truk strikes were flown. For example, one seasoned pilot, upon learning of his next target, confessed to the author many decades later that his first instinct was to jump overboard.

But Truk proved more daunting in reputation than in fact. The operation opened with a spectacular dawn fighter sweep on the 17th, which soon turned into a bitter dogfight involving 70 Hellcats and dozens of Japanese fighters. In the first 20 minutes Lt Cdr Ed Owens' VF-5 from *Yorktown*, supported by elements of 'Fighting 9' and '10', claimed nearly 50 kills. VF-5's boss takes up the story;

'We arrived over the target area with every advantage that could be desired: at dawn, in tactical formation and with the enemy caught by surprise with his aircraft on the ground.

'As we started to strafe airfields, quite a melée developed as the Japs began getting into the air. Actually, there were so many Jap aeroplanes moving that it was almost confusing to select a target and stay with it until it was shot down, without being lured to another target just taking off, or apparently attempting to join up in some kind of formation.

'After a few minutes it was difficult to find uncluttered airspace. Japanese aircraft were burning and falling from every quarter, and many were crashing on take-off as a result of strafing. Ground installations were exploding and burning, and all this in the early golden glow of the dawn. I guess it prompted me to recall it as a "Hollywood war". At times it all looked like it might have been staged for the movies.

'I would say that up until that time, the Truk raid was the greatest "show in town", and I wouldn't have missed it for anything!'

*Intrepid's* 'Fighting Six' was close behind VF-5, and Lt(jg) Alex Vraciu flamed three Zekes and a 'Rufe' floatplane, running his tally to nine. Later

This VF-24 pilot has taken the barrier aboard the light carrier USS *Belleau Wood* after sustaining combat damage over Kwajalein on 1 February 1944. This vessel was one of 12 'flat tops' that made up Task Force 58.2 during the Marshall Islands operation (*Jerry Scutts*)

VF-5 was heavily engaged in combat over Truk Atoll on 17 February 1944, downing 30 of the 124 aircraft claimed on this date. The unit did suffer losses during this bitter fighting, however, F6F BuNo 25761 coming to grief when landing back aboard *Yorktown* the following day

*Intrepid's* VF-6 also enjoyed success on 17 February, claiming 16 kills. This group shot was just prior to the Truk strike occurring, and includes three aces – Lt (jg) Cyrus J Chambers (standing, second from right), who scored 5.333, three on the 17th; Ens Joe D Robbins (middle row, second from left), who finished the war with five, and claimed a Zeke on the 17th; and Lt(jg) Alex Vraciu (to Robbins' left), whose tally reached 19, including four on the 17th. The latter's 'white 32' serves as a backdrop (*via Mark Styling*)

All available deck crew pull together to move the Hellcat up to the bow of the *Essex*. 'Fighting Nine' was the top scoring unit over Truk on the 17th, logging claims for 35 aircraft destroyed (*US Navy*)

that morning, 'Ham' McWhorter of VF-9 claimed two Zekes and a 'Hamp' to become the first pilot to score ten kills in Hellcats. However, VF-18's very capable Don Runyon had already become the Navy's first double ace, having logged his tenth kill of the war (second in F6Fs) on 4 January. Two land-based pilots had also reached double figures by early February – Lt Cdr Tom Blackburn and Lt(jg) Ira Kepford, both of the Corsair-equipped VF-17.

At day's end, Vice Adm Mitscher's fighter pilots had claimed 124 aerial kills, while scores of other enemy aircraft had been attacked on the ground. Approximately 250 of Truk's 365 aircraft had been destroyed or damaged in one frantic day of combat, thus allowing Mitscher's SBDs and TBFs to sink 14 naval vessels and two-dozen merchant ships unopposed from the air. However, there was a price to be paid for this stunning success, as 25 aircraft of the Fast Carrier Task Force were lost, and torpedo damage was sustained by *Intrepid*. Nevertheless, the naval balance in the mid-Pacific had been irrevocably altered.

So too had the pace of Pacific air combat. Between 1 January and 31 March, the number of Navy aces had doubled, which was a phenomenal increase, as the first 25 months of the war had produced fewer than 30 'blue water' aces in total. Yet in the first quarter of 1944, nearly three-dozen Hellcat and Corsair pilots logged their fifth victories, 21 of whom flew F6Fs. The F4U aces came entirely from Lt Cdr Blackburn's land-based VF-17 (for further details see *Aces 8 Corsair Aces of World War 2* by Mark Styling).

Truk was revisited at sunrise on 29 April and, in the words of an *Enterprise* strike leader, 'We wrecked the place!' Primary target this time was

Truk's remaining dockside facilities, as the harbour was nearly devoid of ships. The beneficiary of the dawn sweep was *Langley's* VF-32, led by Lt Cdr Eddie Outlaw. The CO personally gunned five Zekes while his pilots claimed 16 more. Three of those fell to Lt Hollis Hills, a former RAF pilot who, on 19 August 1942, had scored the first victory for the P-51 Mustang when he downed an Fw 190 over the Dieppe beach-head (for further details see *Aces 7 Mustang Aces of the Ninth and Fifteenth Air Forces and the RAF* by Jerry Scutts). Hills later joined the ranks of the aces with his fifth career victory in September 1944. The second Truk was by far the biggest combat in VF-32's career, amounting to half the squadron's score by the end of its deployment.

'Fighting Six' emerged with 19 kills over the big lagoon, and Lt(jg) Alex Vraciu became the Navy's fifth double ace – only the second Hellcat pilot to reach that plateau at that point in the war. His Zekes that morning ran his tally to 11, a score which would increase significantly before much longer.

In all, Task Force 58 pilots claimed 58 kills during the second Truk strike. This bastion would be revisited frequently over the next 16 months, but never again would strikes be opposed by Japanese aircraft in numbers of any consequence.

## ─── 'AN OLD-TIME TURKEY SHOOT' ───

VF-16 pilot Ens Z W 'Ziggy' Neff probably gave the Marianas operation of mid-June its popular name of the 'Turkey Shoot', but to the American planners of the invasion of the mid-Pacific islands, it was known as Operation *Forager*.

Although the strategic aim of seizing the Marianas was to obtain bases for the Army Air Force, the means was amphibious. Marine Corps and Army assault troops would occupy Saipan, Guam and Tinian, but first local air superiority had to be achieved. The only means of doing so was obvious – carrier-based Hellcats.

Vice Adm Mitscher brought 15 fast carriers to the Marianas, deployed in four groups – six *Essexes*, the veteran *Enterprise* and eight of the nine *Independence*-class CVLs. Altogether, the 15 air groups embarked 479 F6F-3s, including 27 radar-equipped -3N night fighters of VF(N)-76 and -77. The 'Big E's' VF(N) detachment comprised three F4U-2 Corsairs, proving how far the concept had come since O'Hare's untimely death less than seven months before.

The air superiority phase began with afternoon fighter sweeps on 11 June. During the day, seven Japanese reconnaissance aircraft were splashed during Task Force 58's approach, including a 'Judy' scout-bomber by VF-50's CO, Lt Cdr J C Strange (his second kill in an eventual tally of five). It became the first of 870 Hellcat victims during the two-month campaign.

Beginning at 1300 that afternoon, elements of 14 Hellcat squadrons began thinning the defenders. Most heavily engaged was VF-2, led by Cdr W A Dean, Jr, who claimed three Zekes and a 'Tojo' over Guam – he finished the war with 11 kills. In all, the *Hornet* pilots were credited with 26 victories, followed by *Cabot's* VF-31. Lt(jg) V A Rieger (five total) claimed three of the 'Meataxers'' 13 kills over Tinian.

Tinian was also home for Naval Air Group 321 – the Japanese night-fighting contingent in the Marianas – who were ordered to fly their Nakajima J1Ns against the task force in a mid-afternoon attack. Cdr W M Collins, Jr, (nine kills) of *Bunker Hill's* VF-8 tackled a batch of 'Irvings' from the unit as they climbed out from their airfield at Gurguan, claiming three himself while Lt(jg) R J Rosen (six kills) bagged two more. By late afternoon TF-58 had claimed 98 confirmed victories, and the Marianas campaign was underway.

Japan's defence against the invasion was two-fold. Firstly, major por-

Three of VF-9's 35 kills fell to Ens John 'Tubby' Franks, Jr, who gunned down two Zekes and a 'Pete' over Truk Lagoon during the unit's first morning sweep of the atoll. He scored his fifth kill five days later over Saipan airfield, and then added a further two victories in 1945 when flying F6F-5s with VF-12. This shot was taken soon after he had made 'ace' on 22 February 1944 (*John Franks via Mark Styling*)

VF-10 'Grim Reapers' also took a heavy toll of the Truk defenders on the 17th, claiming 29 aircraft destroyed and a further 11 damaged. This shot shows two sailors rapidly replenishing the almost obligatory 150-US gal centreline tank of a 'Reapers'' F6F-3 spotted on the stern of USS *Enterprise* during the height of the Truk assault (*US Navy*)

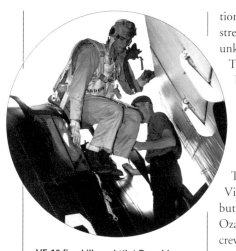

VF-10 five-kill ace Lt(jg) Donald 'Flash' Gordon squeezes out of his cockpit following a patrol over Truk on 16 February – note his personalised N2885 life-jacket (*US Navy*)

VF-32 pilots pose for the camera on *Langley* after completing a sortie over Truk that saw them down 21 Zekes. CO, Lt Cdr Eddie Outlaw (bottom row, second from right), claimed five, his wingman (front row, extreme right), Lt(jg) D E Reeves, four, Lt(jg) R H May (in sunglasses), three, Ens J A Pond (to May's left), two, Lt H H Hills (front row, second from left), three, his wingman (to Hills' right), Lt(jg) L R McEachern, two, and Lt(jg)s H C McClaugherty (behind Hills) and Lt(jg) R A Schulze (to his right), one each

tions of the 61st Air Flotilla were based in the Marianas with a paper strength of some 630 aircraft, although the actual total remains unknown. Despite this considerable force, the Naval General Staff in Tokyo placed even greater stock in the 'second string to their Marianas bow' – Vice Adm Jisaburo Ozawa's First Mobile Fleet, whose nine carriers deployed nearly 440 fighter and attack aircraft. Though smaller than the land-based component, Ozawa's force, with its greater range and mobility, was expected to prove that the balance of power was in favour of the occupying forces.

Although the Japanese boasted a larger number of aircraft than Task Force 58, the decisive factor was qualitative, not quantitative. Vice Adm Mitscher's air groups were, for the most part, not only skilled but experienced. And institutionally, the Fifth Fleet vastly exceeded Ozawa's in every quality. Aside from modern aircraft and competent aircrews, by mid-1944 American radio, radar and operating procedures were thoroughly tested. The battle could only go one way.

But Adm Raymond Spruance was taking no chances. The Fifth Fleet commander directed Mitscher to launch pre-emptory strikes against the Bonin Islands, halfway between Guam and Tokyo, to prevent aerial reinforcements from reaching the Marianas. Therefore, on 15 June Task Groups 58.1 and 58.4 attacked Iwo Jima with three heavy and four light carriers. The result was a series of frantic dogfights beneath rain-laden skies, resulting in widespread combats by VFs -1, -2 and -15. Lt L G Barnard (eight kills) from *Hornet* became an ace in his first fight as VF-2 tallied 17 of the day's 41 claims over 'Iwo'. He reported to the squadron's intelligence officer;

'I would estimate there were 30-40 Zekes in the air when we arrived over the target. We were at 15,000 when I saw several Zekes making runs on some F6Fs below us at 1000 ft. We pushed over after them and, as we did so, we saw eight to ten coming in below us. I made a head-on run on one from above. I turned as I passed to see him blow up. Wings and debris went everywhere.

'I pulled up and missed one and a Zero pulled in front of me at 9000 ft. I fired on him from six o'clock at the same level. He blew up and I went right through his fire.

'After that one, I turned around and there was a Zero on an F6F's tail. I fired a full deflection shot from nine o'clock below, and he blew up. By this time they were blowing up all over the place.

'From there I pulled around until I saw one on the water at about 200 ft altitude. I got it, level at eight o'clock, and it rolled over into the water.

'I climbed back up for altitude to 5000 ft and saw a Zero above me. It was at 8000 ft and making an over-

VF-9 pilots pose with their scoreboard for an end of tour photo on the deck of *Essex* in late February 1944. The 'Hellcats' claimed 120 kills during their second spell in the frontline, and produced ten aces in the process. No fewer than 1332 combat sorties were completed in this 1943/44 tour, and the unit lost one pilot killed in action and four posted as missing – a further seven were lost in non-combat related flying accidents (*Barrett Tillman*)

Grumman aircraft have a reputation for being well-built, and the Hellcat was no exception. This VF-15 F6F-3 had its horizontal tailplanes so badly damaged by AA fire during a strike on the Marcus Island on 20 May 1944 that its pilot was forced to land back aboard *Essex* without the benefit of flaps – with the tails shredded the deployment of the landing aids could have caused the aircraft to stall on approach (*Jerry Scutts*)

Seen during Operation *Reckless* (Hollandia and Aitape landings) in April, the pilot of this VF-2 F6F-3 has opened the canopy to help cool his warm cockpit. Few aircraft were encountered during this op, with the VF-2 downing just a solitary 'Betty' (which fell to Lt(jg) D A Carmichael, Jr, his first of 12 kills) on the 24th

head run on an F6F at 6000. I followed it down to the water. It went into its run and pulled through faster than I did, so I went into a wing-over. Two more F6Fs closed and it turned inside them. Before they could bring their guns to bear, I pulled up in a high wing-over and shot it down from eight o'clock above, 100 ft off the water.'

A pair of *Yorktown's* VF-1 pilots scored four victories each on the 15th – Lt P M Henderson, Jr, and Lt(jg) J R Meharg – although the former, who had just became an ace in this combat, failed to return. His Hellcat was one of 12 US aircraft lost in the two-day neutralisation of Iwo Jima.

American claims were undoubtedly optimistic, but the damage inflicted was genuine. For instance, Japan's Air Group 301 put up 18 Zekes to contest the raid and 17 were lost with 16 pilots killed.

With TF-58 reunited west of Saipan, the largest carrier battle in history began on the morning of 19 June. Ozawa's force had sortied from Borneo six days before, and despite poor communications and scouting, had located Mitscher's four carrier groups and single battleship group and began launching four major raids from its three carrier divisions. The weather favoured Japan – clear skies and an easterly breeze which allowed the Mobile Fleet to continue steaming toward its targets without interrupting flight operations. However, the Americans also knew where to find Ozawa. US submarines had dogged him since he left Tawi Tawi, and

before the battle was fully joined on the 19th, they had torpedoed two of his largest carriers – Pearl Harbor survivor *Shokaku* and his flagship, *Taiho*. In hours both ships had succumbed to their damage.

Of Ozawa's four main strikes, only three had the potential to harm Mitscher. The first was a 64-aircraft raid from three of his smallest carriers – *Chitose, Chiyoda* and *Zuiho*. Alerted by radar, 74 Hellcats from eight squadrons were up and waiting at 1035. Three F6F pilots were

This well-used combat veteran (note the paint-chipped wing leading edges) from VF-2 was photographed aboard *Hornet* on 6 May 1944, having recently been involved in a gunnery sortie judging by the staining under its wings (*Jerry Scutts*)

Double Wasps burbling away, Hellcats of VF-8 are prepared for launch from *Bunker Hill* on D-Day (15 June 1944) for the Saipan landings (*Jerry Scutts*)

Operation *Forager* involved 15 fast carriers, which combined could put aloft an awesome 479 Hellcats to patrol the skies over the Marianas, ensuring the success of the amphibious assault on Saipan, Guam and Tinian. Pilots from VF-1 were involved in this action right from the start, and are seen here heading to their Hellcats aboard *Yorktown* at midday on 15 June 1944. That afternoon the unit was embroiled in dogfights over Iwo Jima that saw them destroy 20 Zekes (*Tailhook*)

killed, including the commander of *Princeton's* Air Group 27, Lt Cdr Ernest Wetherill Wood (who had claimed two Vichy French Dewoitine D.520 fighters whilst flying F4F-4s with VF-41 during Operation *Torch* in November 1942), but 'Raid I' was defeated in detail. The few Japanese pilots to penetrate the combat air patrol wasted their efforts against the battleship group.

'Raid II' registered on US radars about 40 minutes after the first strike. With 109 effective sorties from *Taiho*, *Shokaku* and *Zuikaku*, this strike was the largest of the day. It was also met by the greatest concentration of F6Fs as hard-pressed fighter directors vectored no fewer than 162 Grummans onto the Japanese. *Essex's* highly-proficient VF-15 benefited from being first to intercept both 'Raids' 'I' and 'II', with impressive results – by day's end 'Fighting 15' had claimed 68.5 victories. However, Ozawa's second strike succeeded in penetrating three task groups, attacking one battleship and four carriers, but inflicting minimal damage. In turn, six Hellcats and three pilots were lost in blunting 'Raid II'.

The third Japanese strike put up only 49 aircraft from *Junyo*, *Hiyo* and *Ryuho*, and accomplished nothing. By the time the strike got within range of the US task force at 1300, only 16 Zekes remained in formation. They were mauled by a like number of Hellcats, losing seven A6M5s for no F6Fs shot down.

'Raid IV' was a collaborative venture from Ozawa's Carrier Divisions One and Two. However, only 64 of the 82 aircraft despatched reached the target area, and became further dispersed in ineffective attacks or attempts to land at Guam. The latter were 'greeted' by 41 Grummans from four squadrons at about 1600, and they shot down at least 30 and destroyed a further 20 on the ground. Two F6F pilots were killed in this phase of the battle.

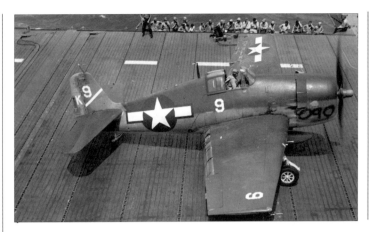

Four days later VF-1 almost doubled its 15 June score when it downed 37 aircraft on the opening day of the Battle of the Philippine Sea – the largest carrier battle in history. Two Zekes (plus a probable third) fell to the pilot of this F6F-3 (BuNo 40090), Lt William C Moseley, although he was flying another Hellcat (BuNo 41438) on the 19th – indeed, the latter machine was so badly damaged in the melée off Iwo Jima that it was pushed over the side of *Yorktown* following his recovery back aboard ship (*US Navy*)

More Combat Air Patrols (CAPs) were flown over the islands that evening, resulting in further combats. *Essex* pilots claimed nine more victories, but their skipper, Cdr C W Brewer (6.5 kills), was lost, along with his wingman.

The 'Turkey Shoot' was a triumph of both technology and training. Including combats during long-range searches, the 15 F6F squadrons had been credited with 371 shootdowns against the loss of 14 pilots. Aside from VF-15, the most successful units were *Lexington's* veteran VF-16 with 46 victories, *Hornet's* VF-2 with 43 and *Yorktown's* VF-1 with 37. *Princeton's* VF-27 was most successful of the CVL units with an even 30 'splashes'.

Wearing the unit's famous 'High Hatters' emblem forward of the windscreen, 'White 5' has its engine throttled up prior to the pilot releasing the brakes and rolling down *Yorktown's* wooden runway on the history-making afternoon of 19 June 1944 (*Aerospace Publishing*)

A combat-damaged tailhook which snapped under the strain of the arrested landing resulted in this late-build F6F-3 gently nosing over upon recovery on *Yorktown* on 19 June (*Jerry Scutts*)

Leading one of the interceptions on 19 June was Lt Cdr Frederick A Bardshar (7.5 kills), who later that day was promoted to command both VF-27 and *Princeton's* air group following the death of his CAG, Cdr E W Wood. Bardshar retained vivid memories of the inbound Japanese strike groups:

'We met a large number of escorted single-engine Japanese bombers while still climbing at about 14,000 ft. I was fascinated by the general inactivity of the Japanese escort fighters, who continued to weave above the bomber formations as the head-on confrontation of Japanese bombers and US fighters occurred.

'A melée followed, one of several. The Japanese escorts did not oppose the intercept, nor were they effective after the melee began. As I recall, I claimed two aircraft. The second, a 'Val', drew me out of the fight by diving, and after he flamed at roughly 7000 ft, the engagement was essentially over. The sky was marked with numerous burning and falling aircraft and some chutes as well as AA over the force.

'Air and communication discipline had been emphasized in VF-27 and was evident in the engagement. Section integrity was, generally, maintained, and transmissions were limited and to the point. We learned,

among other things, that the F6F belly tank was a critical recognition item. Those who jettisoned their tanks were subject to attack by US aircraft from other squadrons.

'The tactics of our principal intercept were not refined, and we were quite vulnerable to the escorting Zeros who had a useable altitude advantage. Having no altitude advantage on the bombers ourselves, we initiated with flat side runs followed by tail chases. My shooting was all no deflection, which I think was typical. The Japanese were unquestionably constrained by fuel limitations.'

Aside from F6Fs, CV-based dive- and torpedo-bombers crews claimed 4.5 victories, and escort-carrier FM Wildcat pilots added four more, running the day's total to 380 credited victories. It remains the greatest one-day tally in the history of American air combat.

Individually, six Hellcat pilots became aces in a day, accruing 34 confirmed victories in total. Three were *Essex* pilots – Cdr David McCampbell, the air group commander, with seven kills in two interceptions; his fighter leader, Cdr Brewer, with five; and Lt(jg) G R Carr with five – the latter went to score 11.5 kills. Two *Hornet* aviators achieved their scores in the traffic pattern over Guam, with Ens W B Webb (seven kills in total), a former enlisted pilot, claiming six confirmed and two probables, while Lt R L Reiserer (nine kills in total) of VF(N)-76 scored five. Lt(jg) Alex Vraciu of VF-16, already the top-scoring carrier aviator at the time, downed six 'Judys' for a total of 18. In the following passage, reproduced with due acknowledgement to *The Hook*, Vraciu describes this combat in detail:

'As part of the American task force protecting the Saipan operation, we were expecting an attack by over 400 Japanese carrier planes on the morning of 19 June 1944. Bogies were up on radar as they approached in several large groups and carrier fighter aircraft were scrambled to supplement the combat air patrols already aloft. I was part of a VF-16 standby group of 12 F6F-3 Hellcat fighters launched from USS *Lexington* (CV-16).

'As we climbed for altitude at full military power, I heard "Sapphire Base", *Lexington*'s Fighter Direction Officer (FDO), as he he broadcast, "Vector 270 (degrees), angels 25, pronto". VF-16 skipper Lt Cdr Paul D Buie led our three divisions

Oil-stained 'White 30' may just be a candidate for 'Davey Jones' locker' judging by the leading-edge damage to the starboard wing sustained in this 19 June crash. A seasoned campaigner, this F6F-3 already sports a replacement rudder (which has suffered combat damage during its latest tussle with the enemy) from a previous close shave (*Jerry Scutts*)

Seen aboard *Lexington* on 13 June, 'White 26' wears six kill markings. As Ralph Hanks pointed out in chapter one, all VF-16 pilots had an 'assigned' aircraft, and it is likely that this F6F belonged to Lt(jg) W E Burckhalter, as he was the only pilot in the unit at this time with exactly six kills. If this is the case, the F6F outlasted its assigned pilot, as Burckhalter had drowned off Saipan 48 hours before, having ditched a flak damaged BuNo 40676

Ens Wilbur 'Spider' Webb of VF-2 made ace on 19 June when he took on a large formation of 'Vals' alone at low-level over Guam, downing six. He made the now famous radio transmission, 'Any American fighter near Orote Peninsula. I have 40 Jap planes surrounded and need a little help', prior to engaging the enemy! Webb's score would have probably been even greater had he not suffered intermittent gun failure (*Wilbur Webb via Mark Styling*)

Soon after Saipan had been secured, ranking Navy ace Cdr David Mc-Campbell replaced his late-build F6F-3, nicknamed *The Minsi*, with this factory-fresh F6F-5, shipped from America. Looking resplendent in its Glossy Sea Blue (FS 25042) scheme, McCampbell's *Minsi II* has its engine and fuel system cleared of inhibitor off Saipan prior to being officially cleared for ops (*Tailhook*)

of four planes each. I led the second division of F6F-3s.

'Overhead, converging contrails of fighters from other carriers could be seen heading in the same direction. After a while, the skipper, who was riding behind a new engine, began to pull ahead steadily until he was out of sight. We had seen his wingman, Lt(jg) W C B Birkholm, drop out – the full-power climb was too much for his engine. Birkholm's propeller froze and he headed downward to a ditching. Luckily, he was picked up by a destroyer 14 hours later.

'My engine was throwing an increasing film of oil onto my windshield, forcing me to ease back slightly on the throttle. My division stayed with me, and two other planes joined us. When I found that my tired engine would not go into high blower, our top altitudewas limited to 20,000 ft. Our predicament was reported to "Sapphire Base".

'All the way up, my wingman, Ens Homer W Brockmeyer, repeatedly pointed toward my wing while observing radio silence. Thinking he had spotted the enemy, I attempted to turn over the lead to him, but each time I tried he would only shake his head. Not understanding what he meant, I finally shook him off in order to concentrate on the immediate task facing us. I found out later that my wings weren't fully locked – the red safety barrels were showing – which explained "Brock's" frantic pointing.

'It was all over before our group reached this particular wave of attacking aircraft, and I was ordered to return my group to the task force and orbit overhead at 20,000 ft. We had barely arrived at our station when the FDO vectored us on a heading of 265 degrees. Something in his voice told us that he had a good one on the string. The bogies were 75 miles away when reported, and we headed outbound in hope of meeting them halfway. I saw two other groups of Hellcats converging off to starboard, four in one group and three in the other.

'About 25 miles out, I tallyhoed three bogeys and closed on them. In the back of my mind, I figured that there had to be more than three as I remembered the seriousness in the FDO's voice. Spot-gazing intently, I suddenly picked out a large, spread-out, mass of at least 50 planes, 2000 ft below us, portside and closing. My adrenalin flow hit high C. They were about 35 miles from our forces and heading in fast. I remember thinking that this could develop into the once-in-a-lifetime fighter pilot's dream.

'Puzzled and suspicious, I looked about for the accompanying enemy fighter cover that normally one would expect over their attacking planes, but none were seen. By this time we were in a perfect position for a high-side run on the enemy aircraft. I rocked my wings as I began a run on the nearest straggler, a *Judy* dive-bomber.

'However, I noted out of the corner of my eye that another F6F seemed to have designs on the same

'Judy' as well. He was too close for comfort and seemed not to see me, so I aborted my run. There were enough cookies on this plate for everyone, I thought. Streaking underneath the formation, I had a good look at the enemy planes for the first time. They were 'Judys', 'Jills' and Zekes. I radioed an amplifying report.

'After pulling up and over, I picked out another 'Judy' on the edge of the formation. It was mildly manoeuvring, and the Japanese rear gunner was squirting away as I came down from behind. I worked in close, gave him a burst and set him afire quickly. The 'Judy' headed for the water, trailing a long plume of smoke.

'I pulled up again to find two more 'Judys' flying a loose wing. I came in from the rear to send one of them down burning. Dipping my Hellcat's wing, I slid over on the other and got it on the same pass. It caught fire also, and I could see the rear gunner continuing to pepper away at me as he disappeared in an increasingly sharp arc downward. For a split second I almost felt sorry for the little bastard.

'That made three down, and we were now getting close to our fleet. Though the number of enemy planes had been pretty well chopped down, many still remained. It didn't look as if we would score a grand slam and I reported this to our FDO. The sky appeared full of smoke and pieces of aircraft as we tried to ride herd on the remaining enemy planes in an effort to keep them from scattering.

'Another meatball broke formation and I slid onto his tail, again working in close due to my inability to see clearly through my oil-smeared windshield. I gave him a short burst, but it was enough. The rounds went right into the sweet spot at the root of his wing. Other rounds must have hit the pilot or the control cables, as the the buring plane twisted crazily out of control.

'Despite our efforts, the 'Jills' started their torpedo runs and the remaining 'Judys' prepared to peel off for their bombing runs. I headed for a group of three 'Judys' flying in a long column. By the time I had reached the tail-ender, we were almost over our outer destroyer screen but still fairly high when the first 'Judy' was about to begin his dive. As he started his nose-over I noticed a black puff appear beside him – our 5-inchers were beginning to open up.

'Trying to disregard the flak, I overtook the nearest enemy bomber. It seemed that I had scarcely touched the gun trigger when his engine began to come to pieces. The 'Judy' started smoking then began torching alternately on and off as it disappeared below me.

'Before I caught up with it, the next 'Judy' was in its dive, apparently trying for one of the destroyers. This time, a short burst produced astonishing results – he blew up in a tremendous explosion in my face. I must have hit its bomb, I guess. I had seen planes explode

Lt Russ Reiserer, CO of the nocturnally-optimised VF(N)-76 Det 2 aboard *Hornet*, was another pilot who made 'ace in a day' during the ''Val'' Fest' over Orate on 19 June, although his 'weapon' on this occasion was a 'straight' F6F-3 rather than a -3N. He had been part of a mixed VF-2/VF(N)-76 sweep despatched in the wake of 'Spider' Webb's strike, and had responded to the latter's call for assistance (*Russ Reiserer via Mark Styling*)

Like Webb, Lt Alex Vraciu of VF-16 claimed six kills on 19 June, although his action took place in the morning almost over the task force. Like the former, who struggled to fire all six of his .50s, Vraciu was mechanically hindered in combat by an engine down on power. This shot was taken moments after he had extricated himself from his F6F, having returned to *Lexington* (*Tailhook*)

Vraciu scored his 19th, and last, kill (a 'Zeke') 24 hours after his spectacular successes over the 'Judys' This official Navy shot shows the then ranking carrier ace climbing out 'his' F6F-3 (BuNo 40467/'White 32') aboard Lexington in late July 1944, the battle-weary Hellcat displaying a full scoreboard, plus an obligatory VF-16 decal (*Tailhook*)

One of the more successful CVL-based fighter squadrons involved in *Forager* was VF-51, assigned to USS *San Jacinto*'s CVLG-51. They claimed 22 victories between 11 June and 25 July, of an eventual total of 50.5 kills for its solitary frontline det. VF-51's sole ace, Lt Bob Maxwell, scored six of his seven kills during the 'Turkey Shoot', including a triple score against Ki 61s on 15 June. This F6F boasts a rare example of nose art in the form of 'snake eye' dice and the name *Little Joe* on its cowling (*Tailhook*)

before, but never like this! I yanked up sharply to avoid the scattered pieces od aircraft and flying hot stuff as I radioed, "Splash number six. There's one more ahead and he diving on a BB (battleship). But I don't think he'll make it".

'Hardly had the words than the 'Judy' caught a direct hit that removed it immediately as a factor to be worried about in the war. He had run into a solid curtain of steel from the battlewagon.

'Looking around, it seemed that only Hellcats were in the sky with me. Glancing back along the route from where we had come, I could see only Hellcats and a 35-mile long pattern of flaming oil slicks.

'In my satisfaction at the day's events, I felt that I had contributed my personal payback for Pearl Harbor. However, this feeling begain to dissipate in a hurry when some of our own gunners tried to shoot me down as I was returning to *Lexington*. Although my IFF was on, my approach was from the right direction and I was making the required two 360-degree right turns, it all didn't seem to matter to some of the trigger-happy gun crews in the heat of this fleet battle.

'I would like to think that the choice words I uttered on the radio stopped all that nonsense, but I know better.'

Lt(jg) Vraciu had used only 360 rounds during this legendary action, downing all six aircraft in under eight minutes. As a result of his success over the 'Judys', Vraciu assumed the mantle of top Navy ace from VF-17's Lt(jg) Ira Kepford, the latter having filled this lofty position since scoring his 16th, and final, victory whilst flying F4U-1A Corsairs in the Solomons on 19 February 1944. Vraciu would retain 'pole position' for a further four months.

Late in the afternoon on 20 June, search aircraft and submarines located Ozawa withdrawing westward. Vice Adm Mitscher, released to pursue the retreating enemy, launched a 300-mile strike from each task group. In all, 227 effective sorties were flown, including 96 by Hellcats. They escorted 131 dive- and torpedo-bombers which caught up with the Japanese fleet about two hours before sunset.

Amid billowing clouds and spectacular flak, Task Force 58's aviators pressed home the attack, opposed by roughly 70 interceptors. Dogfights erupted over each carrier group, and their supporting tankers, with F6Fs claiming 22 victories and seven probables for six losses in return.

Most heavily engaged was the *Lexington* formation, as VF-16 fought to defend its SBDs and TBFs. Alex Vraciu claimed a Zero destroyed and another damaged, running his score to 19 confirmed. Five other fighter squadrons gained victories, most notably *Enterprise's* VF-10 (seven confirmed) and *Wasp's* VF-14 (five over the oilers.) The most successful F6F pilots of the mission were Ens C S Beard (four kills in total) of VF-50, Lt(jg) R C Tabler (three kills in total) of

VF-24, and Ens J L Wolf, Jr (four kills in total), of VF-10, all with double kills.

Avengers from *Belleau Wood* sank the carrier *Hiyo*, and additional damage was inflicted on others, but at a considerable cost. During the long, dark return to the task force, some 70 aircraft succumbed to fuel exhaustion or battle damage. Within this number were 14 F6Fs, which hiked Hellcat attrition on the mission to 20. Task Force 58 had paid a price, but aerial supremacy over the Marianas now was assured.

Iwo Jima had still to be seized, however. In order to keep the pressure on the Bonins, 'Iwo' was 'revisited' on 24 June and 3-4 July. During the first of these strikes, a 10-hour battle was conducted in two parts. A morning fighter sweep resulted in claims for 68 shootdowns by *Yorktown's* VF-1, *Hornet's* VF-2 and *Bataan's* VF-50. Lt(jg) Everett G Hargreaves (8.5 in total) of 'Fighting Two' claimed top honours with five victories. The same three squadrons were largely responsible for another 48 kills in marginal weather later that afternoon.

The two-day repeat performance in July brought another 92 claims, most notably seven credited to a pair of *Hornet* nightfighters in the pre-dawn sweep of the 4th. Lt(jg)s J W Dear, Jr, and F L Dungan (both seven kills in total) of VF(N)-76 were armed with bombs, but stirred up a flock of 'Rufe' floatplanes at Chichi Jima. Although they had emerged from the combat as aces – Dear splashed three 'Rufes' and Dungan four – they had won their laurels the hard way, the former landing just before his engine seized and the latter having suffered a bullet wound.

Dungan's tally was matched by VF-31 pilot Lt(jg) C N Nooy off *Cabot*, who was on his way to becoming the top CVL ace of the war with 19 kills. In all, Task Force 58 added 44 new fighter aces during the month, but even that record would eventually be eclipsed.

No fewer than 28 of the pilots seen in this VF-2 group shot made 'ace' during the 1943/44 combat tour aboard *Hornet*, the unit downing 245 aircraft in a little over nine months – only three 'Red Ripper' pilots were lost in aerial combat in return. A two-thirds life size print of this photograph was used as part of a Navy recruiting exhibition staged in Radio City Music Hall, New York, soon after victory had been clinched in the Marianas (*Connie Hargreaves via Mark Styling*)

As in June, among 'Iwo's' defenders was the hard-pressed Air Group 301, which also took heavy losses in the second series of raids. Partially reinforced, the *hikotai* put up 31 Zeros on 3 July and lost at least 17. Due to the deadly combination of obsolete aircraft flown by inexperienced pilots, the Japanese rate of attrition could only increasing.

The Bonins strike also marked the debut of the ultimate Hellcat, the F6F-5. *Franklin's* VF-13 was the first squadron in the Pacific with a full complement of 'dash fives', which featured the R-2800-10W engine with water-injection as a standard feature. First blood for the new Hellcat was drawn by Lt A C Hudson (one kill in total), whose division claimed three Zekes off Iwo Jima early on the fourth. By the end of the deployment, Cdr W M Coleman (six kills in total) and three of his 'Lucky 13' pilots would be aces in the 'dash five' Hellcat.

From the beginning of *Forager* in mid-June until the middle of August, the Navy added 58 new aces to its ranks, all Hellcat pilots. Therefore, after almost 12 months of combat, the total number of F6F aces stood at 92. That number was about to explode.

**Occupation of the Marianas**

**11 June to 10 August 1944**

| | | |
|---|---|---|
| VF-2 | *Hornet* | 197 |
| VF-15 | *Essex* | 100.5 |
| VF-1 | *Yorktown* | 99 |
| VF-31 | *Cabot* | 67.5 |
| VF-50 | *Bataan* | 58 |
| VF-16 | *Lexington* | 48 |
| VF-8 | *Bunker Hill* | 46 |
| VF-10 | *Enterprise* | 40 |
| VF-14 | *Wasp* | 36.5 |
| VF-27 | *Princeton* | 36 |

**Total by 19 F6F squadrons** — **869.5**

**Top Hellcat Pilots of the Marianas Campaign**

| | | | |
|---|---|---|---|
| Cdr D McCampbell | CAG-15 | 10.5 | Total 34 |
| Cdr W A Dean, Jr | VF-2 | 9 | Total 11 |
| Lt L E Doner | VF-2 | 8 | Total 8 |
| Lt(jg) R T Eastmond | VF-1 | 8 | Total 9 |
| Lt(jg) E C Hargreaves | VF-2 | 8 | Total 8.5 |
| Lt R L Reiserer | VFN-76 | 8 | Total 9 |
| Lt A Van Haren, Jr | VF-2 | 8 | Total 9 |
| Lt(jg) A Vraciu | VF-16 | 8 | Total 19 |
| Lt(jg) J L Banks | VF-2 | 7 | Total 8.5 |
| Lt(jg) D A Carmichael | VF-2 | 7 | Total 12 |

A further 36 F6F pilots claimed five or more victories

# Colour Plates

This 14-page section profiles many of the aircraft flown by the elite pilots of the US Navy, US Marine Corps and the Fleet Air Arm. All the artwork has been specially commissioned for this volume, and profile artist Mark Styling, plus figure artist Mike Chappell, have gone to great pains to illustrate the aircraft, and their pilots, as accurately as possible following in-depth research that included corresponding with over 30 surviving Hellcat aces. Many aces' machines that have never previously been illustrated are featured alongside acccurate renditions of the more famous Hellcats from World War 2.

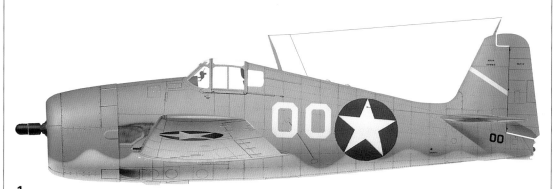

**1**
**F6F-3 white 00/BuNo 04872 of Cdr James H Flatley, CVAG-5, USS *Yorktown*, 6 May 1943**

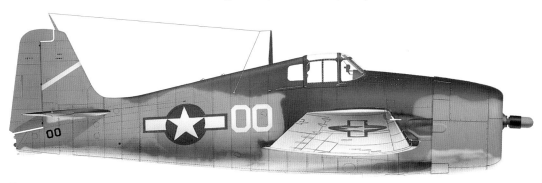

**2**
**F6F-3 white 00 of Cdr James H Flatley, CVAG-5, USS *Yorktown*, 31 August 1943**

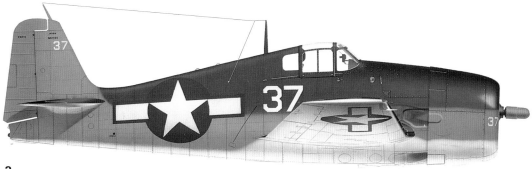

**3**
**F6F-3 white 37/BuNo 08926 of Lt(jg) Eugene R Hanks, VF-16, USS *Lexington*, 23 November 1943**

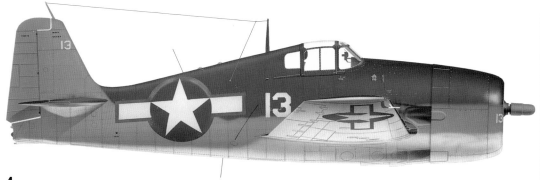

**4**
F6F-3 white 13/BuNo 66064 of Ens Ed 'Wendy' Wendorf, VF-16, USS *Lexington*, 4 December 1943

**5**
F6F-3 white 13 *MY OWN JOAN II*/BuNo 25813 of Lt C K 'Ken' Hildebrandt, VF-33, Ondonga, Christmas Day 1943

**6**
F6F-3 white 22 of Lt(jg) Robert W Duncan, VF-5, USS *Yorktown*, late February 1944

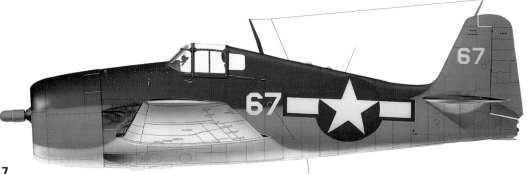

**7**
F6F-3 white 67/BuNo 40381 of Lt Richard 'Rod' Devine, VF-10, USS *Enterprise*, 17 February 1944

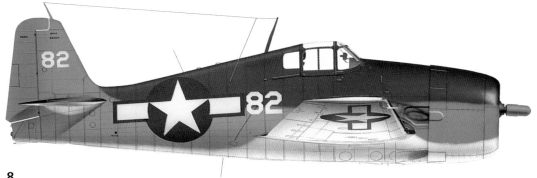

**8**
F6F-3 white 82/BuNo 26183 of Lt(jg) Donald 'Flash' Gordon, VF-10, USS *Enterprise*, 17 February 1944

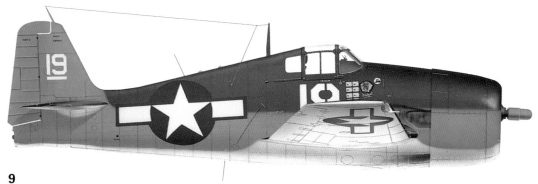

**9**
F6F-3 white 19/BuNo 40467 of Lt(jg) Alexander Vraciu, VF-6, USS *Intrepid*, 17 February 1944

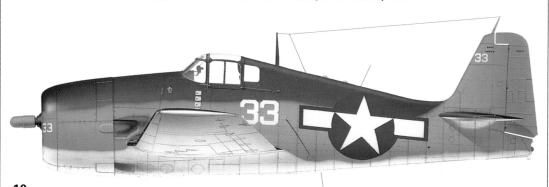

**10**
F6F-3 white 33 of Lt(jg) Frank Fleming, VF-16, USS *Lexington*, April 1944

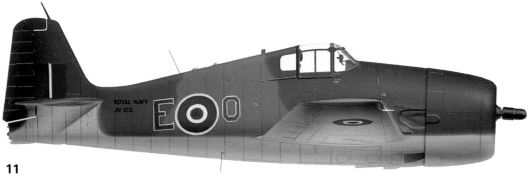

**11**
Hellcat I JV125 of Lt Cdr Stanley G Orr, No 804 Sqn, HMS *Emperor*, 14 May 1944

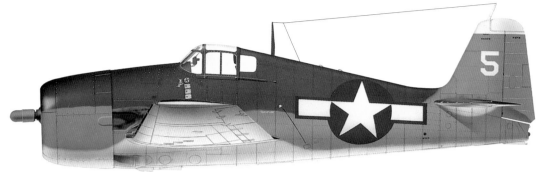

**12**
F6F-3 white 5/BuNo 40315 of Lt Hollis 'Holly' Hills , VF-32, USS *Langley*, 30 April 1944

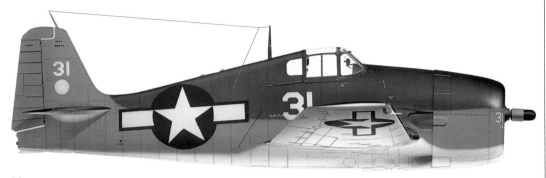

**13**
F6F-3 white 31/BuNo 69532 of Wilbur B 'Spider' Webb, VF-2, USS *Hornet*, 19 June 1944

**14**
F6F-3 *The Minsi* of Cdr David McCampbell, Commander Air Group 15, USS *Essex*, 19 June 1944

**15**
F6F-3 white 36/BuNo 41269 of Ens Wilbur B 'Spider' Webb, VF-2, USS *Hornet*, 20 June 1944

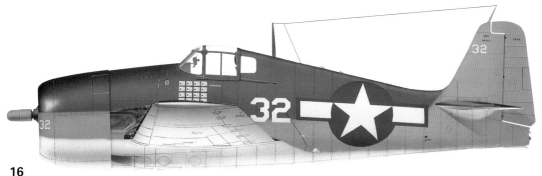

**16**
F6F-3 white 32 of Lt(jg) Alexander Vraciu, VF-16, USS *Lexington*, 21 June 1944

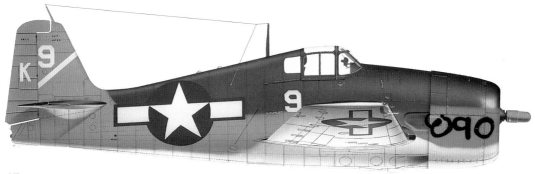

**17**
F6F-3 white 9/BuNo 40090 of Lt William C Moseley, VF-1, USS *Yorktown*, June 1944

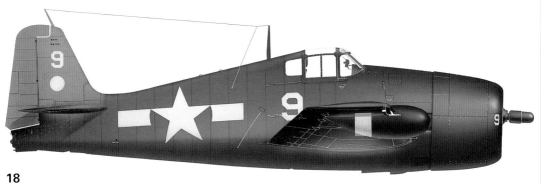

**18**
F6F-3N white 9/BuNo 42158 of Lt Russ Reiserer, VF(N)-76 Det 2, USS *Hornet*, 10 July 1944

**19**
F6F-5 white 8 of Ensigns Alfred R Wood and Edward W Olszewski, VOF-1, USS *Tulagi*, August 1944

**20**
F6F-5 white 12/BuNo 58937 of Lt(jg) Ray 'Hawk' Hawkins, VF-31, USS *Cabot*, September 1944

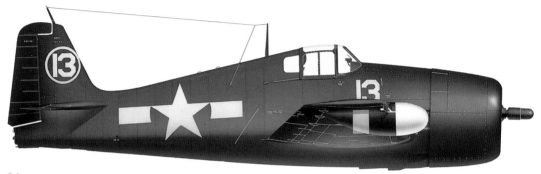

**21**
F6F-5N white 13/BuNo 70147 of Lt William E 'Bill' Henry, VF(N)-41, USS *Independence*, 21 September 1944

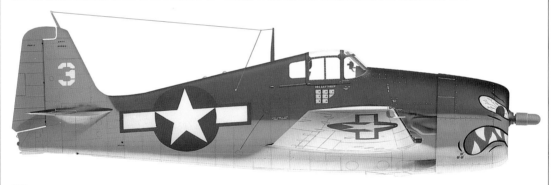

**22**
F6F-3 white 3 of Ens Gordon A Stanley, VF-27, USS *Princeton*, September 1944

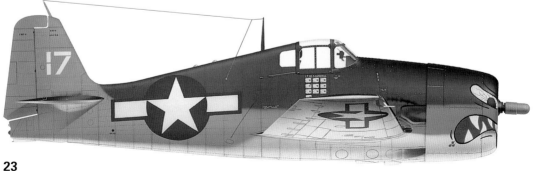

**23**
F6F-3 white 17 of Lt Richard Stambook, VF-27, USS *Princeton*, 24 October 1944

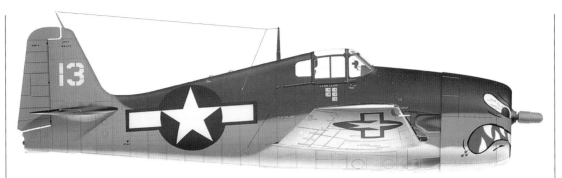

**24**
F6F-3 white 13 of Lt William E Lamb, VF-27, USS *Princeton*, 24 October 1944

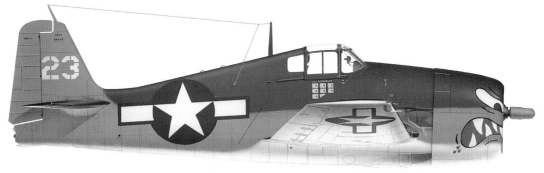

**25**
F6F-3 white 23 of Lt James 'Red' Shirley, VF-27, USS *Princeton*, 24 October 1944

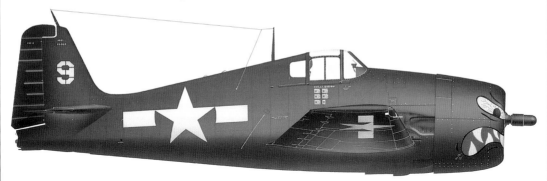

**26**
F6F-5 white 9 of Lt Carl A Brown, Jr, VF-27, USS *Princeton*, 24 October 1944

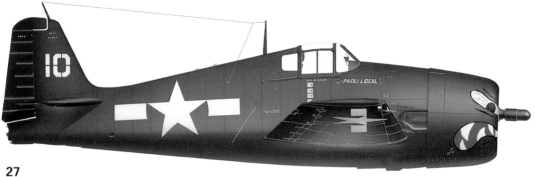

**27**
F6F-5 white 10 *PAOLI LOCAL* of Ens Paul E Drury, VF-27, USS *Princeton*, 24 October 1944

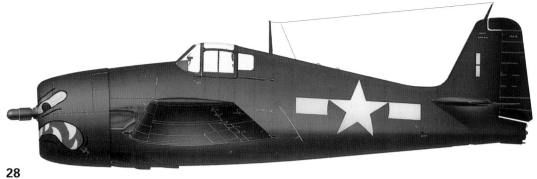

**28**
F6F-5 white 1 of Lt Cdr Fred A Bardshar, CO of VF-27/Commander Air Group 27, USS *Princeton*, 24 October 1944

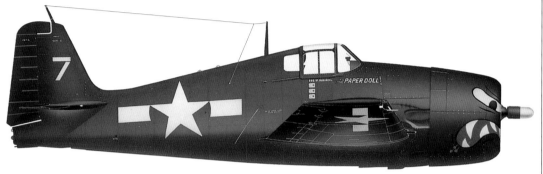

**29**
F6F-5 white 7 *PAPER DOLL* of Ens Bob Burnell, VF-27, USS *Princeton*, 24 October 1944

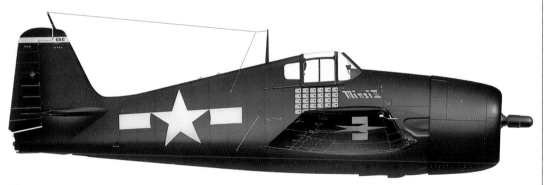

**30**
F6F-5 *Minsi III*/BuNo 70143 of Cdr David McCampbell, Commander Air Group 15, USS *Essex*, 25 October 1944

**31**
F6F-5 white 28/BuNo 58069 of Ens Frank 'Trooper' Troup, VF-29, USS *Cabot*, 29 October 1944

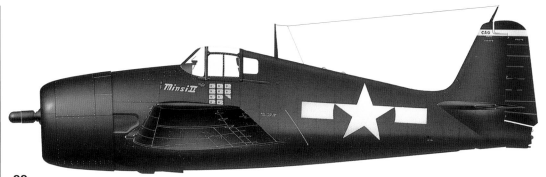

**32**
F6F-5 *Minsi II* of Cdr David McCampbell, Commander Air Group 15, USS *Essex*, October 1944

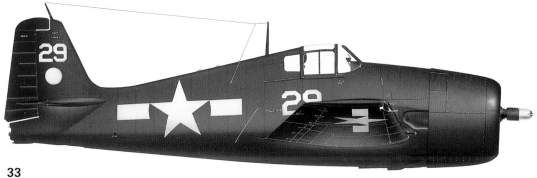

**33**
F6F-5 white 29 of Lt James S Swope, VF-11, USS *Hornet*, October 1944

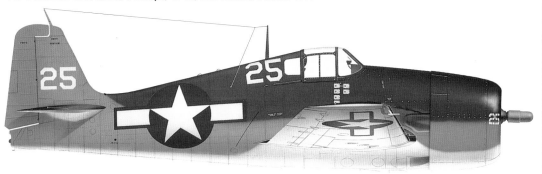

**34**
F6F-5 white 25 of Lt Bruce Williams, VF-19, USS *Lexington*, October 1944

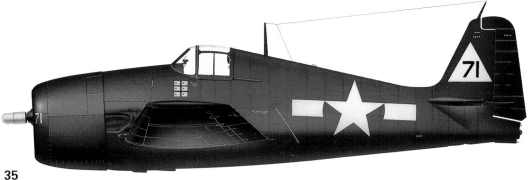

**35**
F6F-5 white 71 of Lt Leo B McCuddin, VF-20, USS *Enterprise*, October 1944

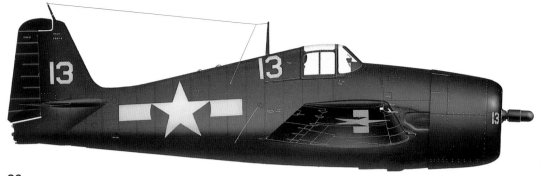

**36**
F6F-5 white 13/BuNo 42013 of Lt(jg) Ed Copeland, VF-19, USS *Lexington*, 6 November 1944

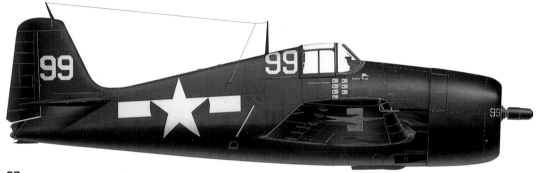

**37**
F6F-5 white 99 of Cdr T Hugh Winters, Jr, Commander Air Group 19, USS *Lexington*, November 1944

**38**
F6F-5 white 9 of Lt Charles 'Skull' Stimpson, VF-11, USS *Hornet*, November 1944

**39**
F6F-5 white 30/BuNo 70680 of Lt(jg) Blake Moranville, VF-11, USS *Hornet*, January 1945

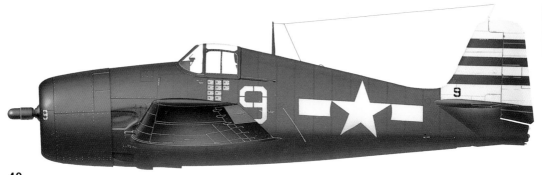

**40**
F6F-5 white 9 of Lt Hamilton McWhorter, III, VF-12, USS *Randolph*, January 1945

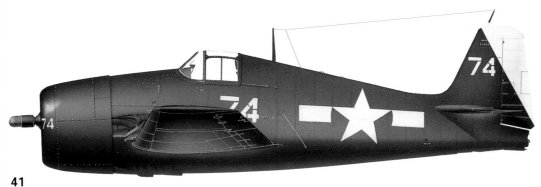

**41**
F6F-5 white 74/BuNo 72354 of Lt John M Wesolowski, VBF-9, USS *Yorktown*, 11 April 1945

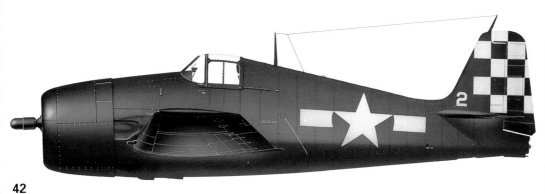

**42**
F6F-5 white 2 of Lt Cdr Robert A Weatherup, VF-46, USS *Independence*, 15 April 1945

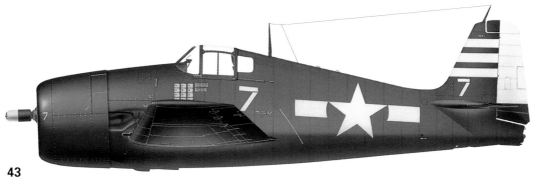

**43**
F6F-5 white 7 of Ens Robert E Murray, VF-29, USS *Cabot*, April 1945

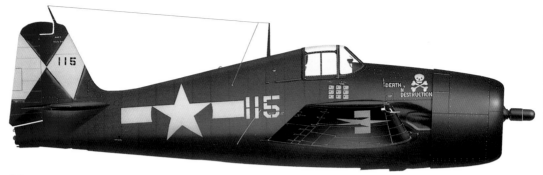

**44**
F6F-5 white 115 *DEATH N' DESTRUCTION*/BuNo 72534 of Ensigns Donald McPherson, Bill Kingston, Jr, and Lyttleton Ward, VF-83, USS *Essex*, 5 May 1945

**45**
F6F-5N white F(N)76/BuNo 78669 of Maj Robert B Porter, VMF(N)-542, Okinawa, 15 June 1945

**46**
F6F-5N black F(N)4/BuNo 78704 of Capt Robert Baird, VMF(N)-533, Okinawa, June 1945

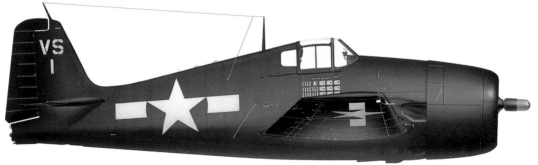

**47**
F6F-5 white VS 1 of Lt Cdr Willard E Eder, 'Victory Squadron', late 1945

**1**
Lt Cdr Paul D Buie, CO of VF-16 aboard USS
*Lexington* in November 1943

**2**
Lt(jg) Alex Vraciu of VF-16 aboard
USS *Lexington* on 19 June 1944

**3**
Lt Jim Swope of VF-11 aboard USS
*Hornet* in January 1945

**4**
Lt Cdr Stanley Orr, CO of No 804 Sqn on HMS
*Emperor* in April 1944

**5**
CAG-15 Cdr David McCampbell
aboard USS Essex in November 1944

**6**
Maj Bruce Porter, CO of VMF(N)-
542, on Okinawa in June 1945

# TO THE PHILIPPINES

American grand strategy in the Pacific was decided at a conference in the summer of 1944. Gen Douglas MacArthur, Adm Chester Nimitz and the members of the Joint Chiefs of Staff chose to reoccupy the Philippine Islands rather than strike toward the Chinese mainland.

Sixteen fast carriers departed Eniwetok Atoll at the end of August with some 520 Hellcats. The ever-increasing requirement for fleet defense had resulted in big-deck carriers embarking up to 54 fighters – a significant increase over the previous 36.

Although depicting F6F-5Ns of US-based VF(N)-107 in August 1944, this shot does show the unique twin 20 mm cannon arrangement fitted exclusively to a modest number of nightfighter Hellcats – the gun barrels on these aircraft lack the cone-shaped flash suppressers worn by their frontline brethren (*US Navy*)

By the time of the Second Battle of the Philippine Sea, the nightfighter concept had progressed from flight-size dets aboard fast carriers, to a dedicated air group tasked with defending TF-38 after dark. CVLG-41 flew night intercepts and bombing missions between August 1944 and January 1945 from the CVL USS *Independence*. Here, VF(N)-41 F6F-5Ns lining up for launch at dusk during the Leyte Gulf action (*Tailhook*)

Thus, the stage was set for the Battle of Leyte Gulf which, if not actually the largest naval engagement of modern times, was certainly the most diverse and intense. In numbers of combatant ships engaged, the Second Battle of the Philippine Sea ran a close second to the 1916 Battle of Jutland. However, for variety and concentration of forces engaged – air, surface and submarine – no other action could match it.

During initial sweeps over Mindanao on 9-10 September, the fast carriers not only surprised a major land-based airpower, but achieved outright aerial supremacy. There was little aerial combat (only 13 shootdowns credited), but enemy airfields were bombed and strafed almost with impunity. It took three days for the Japanese to recover their poise, with the task force experiencing no serious opposition until the 12th.

The first and last of the 82 victories credited that day were claimed by a new, innovative, Hellcat squadron – Lt Cdr T F Caldwell's VF(N)-41. Flying from *Independence*, Caldwell's fighter and torpedo squadrons were wholly devoted to nocturnal interception, strike and interdiction missions. It was a bold experiment, as Caldwell's command was entrusted with proving the concept of a dedicated night air group flying from the narrow deck of a CVL. More would be heard from CVLG(N)-41 during the Philippines campaign.

A mid-morning fighter sweep over Cebu stirred up considerable opposition for VF-15 and -19, team mates in Task Group 38.3. The *Essex* fighter skipper, Lt Cdr J F Rigg (11 kills in total), claimed four

This impressive victory tally and bomb log denotes the career stats of Texan Lt(jg) Ray 'Hawk' Hawkins, second-ranking ace of VF-31 'Flying Meataxes' with 14 kills. The unit produced 14 aces during World War 2, and was credited with the destruction of 165.5 aircraft (*Ray Hawkins via Mark Styling*)

One of the most famous markings ever worn on a US combat aircraft, the ferocious cat's mouth applied by VF-27 to its F6F-3s and -5s was conceived by Lts Carl Brown (10.5 kills, front row fifth from left) and Dick Stambook (10 kills, standing fourth from right), and Ens Bob Burnell (four kills, to Stambook's right) whilst the unit was working up at NAS Kahului, Hawaii, in March/April 1944. Burnell hand-painted 'teeth' on all 24 F6Fs prior to embarking aboard USS *Princeton* on 29 May 1944 (*Paul Drury via Mark Styling*)

Zekes and a 'Tojo' to lead 'Fabled 15's' tally of 27 victories. Meanwhile, 'Satan's Kittens' off *Lexington* bagged 23, including three by the VF-19 CO himself, Cdr T H Winters, Jr (eight kills in total), while Lt Albert Seckel, Jr (six kills in total), went one better by claiming four Zekes.

Most of the remaining shootdowns went to *Hornet* and *Wasp* Hellcats, a number of claims by 'Bombing Fourteen' pilots who had hastily transitioned to fighters. The latter reflected the increasing need for F6F squadrons to meet expanded operations schedules. While many SB2C Helldiver pilots welcomed the chance to switch to Hellcats, the major drawback of such transitions was limited opportunity to acquaint bomber pilots with aerial gunnery and fighter tactics. Nevertheless, the VB-14 aviators did well, and on the 12th five of them combined to score eight kills over Negros Island. At least one VB-2 pilot (Lt(jg) M H Richey) in *Hornet* also shot down an aircraft (a Zeke) whilst flying a Hellcat during this period.

On 13 September nearly 100 claims, including two dozen by VF-31, were added to the F6F tally. Twenty-one-year-old Lt(jg) Arthur R Hawkins (14 kills in total) became only the second CVL 'instant ace' as the *Cabot* pilot downed five Zekes over Negros Island.

Reinforced to a strength of 60 A6M5s, Naval Air Group 201 absorbed the brunt of the combat. Based at Nichols Field and Mactan, it lost four-fifths of its strength in the air or on the ground. Included in the casualties were 10 experienced warrant-officer and NCO pilots.

*Princeton's* ever-aggressive VF-27 emerged with the highest score on 21 September, claiming 37 kills in the Manila area. Top honours belonged to Lt John R Rodgers, who came achingly close to acedom with 4.50 victories (all Ki 61 'Tonys') – his only score of the war.

Leading one of two fighter sweeps from six CVLs was VF-27 CO, Lt Cdr Fred Bardshar. He recalled;

'My group attacked Nichols and Neilsen Fields at Manila with 48 F6Fs. We were stacked in three sub-groups: *Princeton's* at 12,000 ft, 16 others at 16,000 and 16 more at 20,000. We arrived over the target without opposition and my wingman and I initiated action by shooting down a "Nick" over Neilsen at about 10,000 ft. We fired as a section from a high side run. The Jap did not see us. The 12 .50 cal machine guns registered on the first burst with sensational effect. Our targets included parked aircraft at Nichols and Neilsen and also on Dewey Boulevard. I had my right aileron and tailhook shot out and was diverted to a large deck carrier for a barrier arrestment.'

Despite Lt Rodgers' poor luck, three other pilots became aces in a day on the 21st, including two VF-18 aviators off *Intrepid* – Lt Harvey P Picken (11 in total) and Lt(jg) Charles Mallory (10 in total) each splashed five (a combination of 'Bettys' and assorted fighters) whilst flying F6F-5P photo-recce Hellcats.

Picken had two previous kills to his credit but Mallory had never scored before. Meanwhile, VF-31's Lt(jg) Cornelius Nooy was already an ace when he led his division against Clark Field. Attacked by a mixture of enemy fighters, he kept his 500-lb bomb on its rack whilst he gunned down four bandits and flew a fifth into the ground (two Zekes, two 'Tojos' and a 'Tony'). He then proceeded to put his bomb into a hangar on the the ex-USAAF base, and thus finish off one of the finest naval fighter missions flown in World War 2.

Cdr Dean's VF-2 finished its lengthy tour with a final combat on 22 September. 'The Rippers'' last victim (a 'Tony') fell to Ens Wilbur B Webb, the Pearl Harbor survivor who on 19 June had downed six 'Vals' over Guam. The squadron had scored 245 credited victories since November 1943, producing 24 aces in the process.

On 24 September *Essex's* CAG, Cdr McCampbell, shot down a 'Pete' floatplane with his wingman, Lt(jg) Roy W Rushing (13 kills in total). Having previously scored 18.5 victories, McCampbell was now tied with Alex Vraciu, late of VF-16, who had been the Navy's top ace since 19 June.

Then on 21 October CAG-15 shot down a 'Dinah' reconnaissance aircraft and a 'Nate' fighter near Tablas Island, thus running his score to 21 confirmed, setting three records in the process. McCampbell became not only the Navy's top fighter ace, but also the first US Navy pilot, and carrier aviator, to attain 20 victories – he was never seriously challenged for top spot for the duration of the war. It took some time for the news to spread, as Alex Vraciu, who had been the fast carriers' leading ace since late April, recalls;

'We didn't really know much about how the other fellows were doing at the time. You went out, flew some hops, maybe shot down some planes, and then came back. I don't think I knew that Dave had passed me until I rejoined the *Lexington* late that fall.'

Among the fighter squadrons quietly building steady scores was Lt Cdr Fred Bakutis' (7.5 kills) VF-20. Entering combat in August, the new *Enterprise* squadron had to wait until mid-October for its first chance to tackle the enemy. Even then, the honour went to Cdr J S Gray, Jr (six kills in total), recently skipper of VF(N)-78, who flamed a prowling 'Betty' on the night of 11 October – by this stage in the war the formerly independent nightfighter units had been absorbed into the *Essex*-class FitRons.

The following day, VF-20, led by CAG Cdr Dan Smith, Jr (6.083 kills in total), destroyed 21 bandits over Formosa.

Prior to tackling the still-potent Japanese fleet in Philippine waters, Task Force 38 moved to secure its southern flank. The three-day operation aimed at beating down Japanese airpower in Formosa resulted in heavy combat on 12-14 October as carriers again went head-to-head with land-based aviation. And, as before, the carriers won.

Pre-war Warner Brothers actor Lt Bert DeWayne Morris scored five of his seven kills over Leyte Gulf. He appeared in a number of films before entering the Navy in June 1941. Morris returned to Hollywood after the war, starring in Westerns and other films, but retained his naval links through the reserve. In 1959, whilst visiting his old CAG, Capt David McCampbell (who was then commanding the carrier USS *Bon Homme Richard*), Morris died of a heart attack at the age of 45

This photograph, taken on the morning of 21 October 1944, shows CAG-15 David McCampbell taxying forward to his shutdown spot on *Essex* after completing a sweep over Tablas Island, in the Philippines, He had downed a 'Dinah' and a 'Nate' during this sortie, thus assuming the mantle of the US Navy's ranking carrier ace from Alex Vraciu of VF-16 (*Tailhook*)

With the klaxon ringing in their ears, steel-helmeted pilots of VF-20 run for their 5-in rocket-armed F6F-5s aboard *Enterprise* between strikes on Manila on 15 October 1944. Aside from the deck crew tasked with arming the Hellcats and strapping in their pilots, most other sailors seem to be busy scouring the sky off to starboard for an incoming raid of Japanese suiciders – this action off Luzon marked the debut of the *kamikaze* (*US Navy*)

An ex-VF-10 four-kill combat veteran from the 'Grim Reapers'' Wildcat tour of 1942/43, Lt Ed 'Whitey' Feightner was well into his second spell in the frontline – this time with VF-8 aboard *Bunker Hill* – when he claimed his last trio of kills (three Zekes over Taien Airfield, on Formosa) on 12 October 1944, thus bringing his wartime score to nine (*Ed Feightner*)

Early on the 12th, VF-15 and -19 conducted a series of hard-fought combats over the Chinese island. *Lexington's* 'Satan's Kittens' claimed 27 shootdowns while Hellcats from *Essex* bagged 23 more. Their opponents were a mixture of Japanese army and navy types – mainly Zekes, 'Tojos' and 'Oscars'.

Most heavily engaged was 'Fighting Eight', which tore into a formation of 'Nicks', Zekes and 'Oscars' near Taien Airfield. The *Bunker Hill* squadron left 30 aircraft destroyed before returning to the task force. The CO, Cdr William M Collins, Jr (nine kills in total), led the list with four fighters and a bomber, but Ens Arthur P Mollenhauer of VF-18 – barely aged 20 – matched the 33-year-old Collins. It was the youngster's only score, however, as he went missing in action two weeks later after damaging a Zeke whilst flying F6F-5 BuNo 58409 over Luzon.

Most of the shooting was over by early afternoon. Portions of at least 14 carrier air groups had participated in seizing air superiority from the Japanese, with victory claims running at 224 destroyed and 27 probables. *Hancock's* VF-7 recorded its first five victories on this notable day, whilst 24 hous later its CO, Lt Cdr Leonard Check, began damaged an 'Oscar' – he would achieve the status of double ace before the end of the deployment. Only 37 Japanese aircraft were reported shot down on the 13th, largely by *Enterprise's* VF-20 and *Belleau Wood's* VF-21.

The enemy bounced back on 14 October as 92 shootdowns were credited to TF-38 aviators. Over half the claims went to VF-11, -18 and -27. The 'Sundowners' pilots, badly outnumbered by inbound raiders, claimed 14 kills against three pilots and four aircraft lost as Lt Charles Stimpson – already a six-kill Guadalcanal ace in F4Fs – became the squadron's second ace in a day, claiming three 'Hamps' and two Zekes confirmed, and two 'Tonys' as probables. *Princeton's* VF-27, the prominent CVL squadron in the 'Turkey Shoot' four months before, splashed 11 twin-engine 'Fran' bombers offshore.

In exchange for about 30 Hellcats, the Formosa strikes deprived Japan of some 350 aircraft. For the moment, the path to Leyte Gulf was clear.

During this timeframe – mid-September to mid-October – an *Intrepid* pilot had quietly, and competently, been running up an exceptional record. Lt Cecil E Harris of VF-18 had scored one victory as a land-based F4F pilot with VF-27 in the Solomons on 1 April 1943, but now, almost 18 months later, he had finally hit his stride, and in just three combats in 32 days shot down 11 Japanese aircraft – four fighters (three 'Hamps' and a Zeke) on 13 September; two bombers (a 'Sally' and a 'Lilly') and two Zekes on 12 October; and three 'Judys' on the 14th. Still more was yet to come.

On 16 October, *Cabot's* new VF-29 announced itself in spectacular fashion. Lt Cdr Willard E Eder's (6.5 in total) squadron was tasked with 'capping' two American cruisers which had been torpedoed. Japanese bombers pressed hard to finish off the cripples, resulting in VF-29 claiming 34 shootdowns, with Lt Albert Fecke (seven in total) and his number four man, Ens Robert Buchanan (five in total), each destroying five attackers – mainly 'Frans' and 'Jills'. Although USS *Houston* was torpedoed a second time, both cruisers were towed to safety.

Two days later Lt Edward B Turner (seven in total) became *Wasp's* sole instant ace during a dogfight over Mabalacat airfield, claiming four Zekes and an 'Oscar' in VF-14's total score of 16 kills.

## LEYTE GULF

The Battle of Leyte Gulf (also called the Second Philippine Sea) involved nearly 550 Hellcats from the 17 carriers of Task Force 38, plus 65 more embarked in three Task Force 77 escort carriers. The battle began on 24 October with simultaneous strikes by both sides against Japanese fleet units west of the archipelago and US forces to the east.

From 270 claimed shootdowns by US carrier aircraft, an incredible nine instant aces in a day were crowned, including two FM-2 pilots flying from escort carriers. The seven Hellcat aces represented three squadrons, the first being *Lexington's* VF-19 which launched fighter sweeps over Luzon. 'Satan's Kittens' stirred up a variety of bandits, and claimed 30 victories around Luzon, paced by Lt William J Masoner, Jr (12 in total). Already an ace, the former VF-11 pilot more than doubled his wartime total by downing six twin-engined bombers around 0730. In his combat report Masoner wrote;

'My division was escorting four SB2Cs on a 300-mile search. As we came up to join them over the eastern shore of Luzon, they spotted a group of "Bettys" and I saw them shoot down two. I saw four or five "Bettys" scattering in all directions, so I picked one and went down on it with my division. I opened with a quartering shot and rode up on his tail. I observed his 20 mm gun firing from his turret. My incendiaries hit his fuselage and right wingroot. He burst into flame and hit the water.

'I pulled up and saw eight "Dinahs" about 100 ft over me. They turned and spread slightly. I came up from below the right-hand plane and put a long burst into his starboard engine. It started to burn—the flames spread and it fell a mass of flames.

'By this time no more planes were available so we rendezvoused and continued our search. After abut 50 miles one of the bombers tally-hoed two "Nells". We dove down after them and chased them five or six miles. I dropped my bomb and then caught up with them. I made a run from above and astern and his right wing burned, exploded and fell off. He dove into the water and burned. I started to make a run on the other "Nell" but he was already burning and crashed. My wingman got him.

'We then joined the SB2Cs, flew our cross leg and started home. As we approached the shoe of Luzon we spotted five "Nells" at about 500 ft. My wingman and I went down on them and he burned one which crashed. His guns then stopped and he pulled up. I made a high quartering run on one "Nell" and observed hits. I did a wing-over and came up under his tail to avoid his ball turret, which was firing. I hit him in the fuselage at very close range. He exploded and pieces flew all over. He nosed straight down and hit the water.

'I came up from behind and above one the next "Nell" and, hit in the

VF-20's Lt(jg) Melvin 'Pritch' Prichard claimed 2.25 of his 5.25 kills over Manila Bay on 15 October, but perhaps his most daring victory was claimed two days earlier – although it has never been officially credited to him. 'Pritch' downed a 'Betty' at low-level well within TF-38's inner flak cordon, the bomber catching fire and crashing just several hundred feet away from his carrier (*Steven Prichard via Mark Styling*)

Leading VF-11 ace Lt Charles R 'Skull' Stimpson poses for an official photograph in a 'Sundowners'' F6F-5 specially adorned with his final combat tally of 16 kills and an appropriate unit decal. He was without a doubt one of VF-11's most experienced pilots, having made ace in F4Fs over Guadalcanal (*US Navy*)

A VF-29 Hellcat is prepared for a catapult launch from *Cabot* on 10 October 1944. On this date the squadron scored its first victories when future 5.5-kill ace Lt Bruce D Jaques and Ens Frank A Wier downed a pair of twin-engined bombers in an early-morning interception. The former had opened his account back in November 1942 when he downed a Vichy French Bloch 174 or Potez 63/11 whilst flying a Wildcat with VGF-29 (VF-29's previous designation) from USS *Santee* during the *Torch* landings

VF-11's Guadalcanal tour in 1943 produced a number of outstanding pilots who went on to compile big scores in F6Fs. One of these individuals was Lt William J Masoner, Jr, who, upon returning to the US, was sent to VF-19 to help the unit get up to speed tactically. Once his the squadron entered the fray in mid-1944, he showed that he hadn't lost the 'combat edge', and when Masoner departed VF-19 in December, he left it as top ace with 10 F6F kills

wingroot, he exploded, throwing large pieces by me as I pulled up. He burned and crashed.'

Masoner's wingman, Lt(jg) W E Copeland, ran his own tally from three to six and reflected, 'Mr Masoner always found a way to get me into trouble'. Copeland may have set a record for diversity, as his six victories represented six aircraft types – 'Val', 'Oscar', 'Nate', 'Nell', 'Betty' and 'Lily'.

An hour after VF-19 tied into the Japanese bombers, *Princeton's* VF-27 engaged a variety of single-engine fighters over Polilo Island in Lamon Bay, off Luzon's east coast. Twelve of Lt Cdr Fred Bardshar's highly-capable pilots splashed 36 bandits, with Ens T J Conroy (seven in total) claiming six, while Lts J A 'Red' Shirley and C A Brown, Jr, and Lt(jg) E P Townsend, all bagged five apiece – the latter pilot's only kills.

Upon return to TG-38.3 around 0940, the victorious Hellcat pilots were shocked to find their ship aflame. 'Sweet P' had taken two bombs through the flight deck, and fires raged out of control. She was abandoned and scuttled – the first American fast carrier sunk in two years, and the last ever.

VF-27's Ens Paul E Drury was to feel the highs and lows of combat on this fateful day, making ace trying to repel the huge morning attack against the task force, and then having to 'jump ship' when *Princeton* was mortally damaged;

'My greatest and most dramatic exposure to the Battle of Leyte Gulf occurred all wrapped up in one day – 24 October 1944, the longest day of my life. Actually, I guess it started the night before on the evening of the 23rd, as the Japanese had all kinds of observation planes out trying to locate our task force. In fact, I think they already had us located, and they were just keeping track of us until the next morning when they were going to attack.

'Our task group comprised two large carriers, the *Essex*, which was Adm Sherman's flagship, and the *Lexington*, with Vice-Adm Mitscher aboard, the fast carriers *Princeton* and *Langley*, the battleships *Massachusetts* and *South Dakota*, the cruisers *Birmingham*, *Reno*, *Mobile* and *Sante Fe* and 13 destroyers.

'Eight of us from VF-27 were told that evening that we would have CAP duty the next morning, and that we could expect a lot of activity. So we were awakened on the 24th at about 4.00 am, and it was still dark when we took off. Due to a combination of the excitement on the flightdeck, the blacked-out carrier and the fact that we were in a hurry to get off because there were already bogies on the radar screen, I didn't get to fly in my regular plane, the *PAOLI LOCAL*, nor did I get to fly in my regular division (led by Lt Carl Brown, Jr, who bagged five Zekes in this sortie to take his score to 10.5 kills, Ed.).

'I found myself as wingman on Jim "Red" Shirley, who was the leading ace in our squadron (as mentioned earlier, he was to see his score rise from 7.5 to 12.5 kills during the course of the sortie, Ed.). But this was no big deal because I thought as soon as the sun came out I'd slide over to where I belonged, and still maintaining radio silence, I would signal for that pilot to get back where he belonged. That scenario, however, never came to pass, because as soon as we had rendezvoused after take-off the four of us were vectored out on a bogie, which we quickly took care of. As soon as we got back on station, Carl Brown's division of four was vectored out onto a contact, and so the routine continued – I never did get back into my regular division (two *Nicks* were downed in these fleeting battles, one apiece to "Red" Shirley and Ens Robert Blyth, Ed.).

'Following these snooper intercepts all eight of us were given a vector to go on at full speed to tackle a larger formation of aircraft, and as Carl Brown's section had tackled the last snooper, we had a height advantage over his division going into the dogfight. We duly spotted the enemy first, and as the sun had now fully risen, I could clearly see just how large this attack was.

'"Red" Shirley quickly radioed back to *Princeton*, "Tally-ho – Eighty Jap planes", and then thoughtfully added, "better send help".

'The carrier responded "Affirmative", and stated that they could send another 12 fighters to help out, plus contact *Essex* to launch a few more. Our job on CAP was to make sure that the enemy didn't get close to the task force. At this point in the mission we were about 60 to 70 miles away from the carriers, and as our job was to protect the fleet, we really had little choice as to what to do next – we just hoped that those planes being launched would hurry up and get here. However, I knew that it would take quite some time for the fighters to be made reading for take-off and then launched, but it was nevertheless a comforting feeling knowing that help was on its way.

'With this thought firmly in mind, the four of us dived into this Japanese formation. I think that we each downed one plane on that first pass, then after that all hell broke loose and it was just one huge mass of aeroplanes trying to see who could shoot who down. I think the four of us shot down 15 Jap planes that morning (the division's score was officially recorded as 14, with Drury bagging two Zekes and a "Tojo", Shirley a "Nick", a Zero and three "Tojos" and Ens Thomas J Conroy three Zekes and three "Tojos" – the fourth member of the flight remains anonymous, Ed.), and then we were out of ammunition and short on fuel, so we were ordered back to the task force.

'I believe I was one of the last pilots to land on the *Princeton* before it was bombed, as I had just gotten out of my plane and returned to the ready-room for a debrief when a tremendous volume of black

Toting a full complement of rockets, a contrailing VF-7 Hellcat departs USS *Hancock* for a raid on Clark Field on 29 October. High Velocity Aerial Rockets (HVARs) were widely used on F6Fs, being launched from 'zero length' rails beneath the wings. A full load of six gave the Hellcat a weight of fire equivalent to a destroyer's broadside. The original HVARs possessed 3.5-in warheads, but in 1944 the 5-in variety became available. With extraordinary penetrative ability, the ogive warheads could easily puncture the steel plates of most ships, and were also effective against some types of bunkers. The weapon's major drawback was inaccuracy, requiring a long, straight, approach to the target (*Tailhook*)

smoke came billowing into the compartment through the ventilating system. An announcement was soon made that yes indeed we had been bombed, and that all aviators were ordered up to the flightdeck to stand beside their aeroplanes – I think the captain had at first thought that we might be able to launch, but the bomb had gone through the deck and exploded in the hangar bay.

'Unfortunately, just at that moment all our our torpedo planes were below decks being armed and fuelled up, and one solitary bomb that wouldn't have normally done all that much damage, started a chain reaction of destruction. One of the torpedoes exploded and blew up the aft elevator right near where I was standing beside my Hellcat on the flight deck, whilst another took out the forward elevator. The captain immediately realised it was time to abandon ship and instructed all crew, other than the fire control party, to do so. I went over the side down a rope, and swam over to the destroyer *Irwin*, where I collapsed from exhaustion. After surviving another air raid, my "new" ship was ordered to finish *Princeton* off with torpedos, but the two launched failed to hit the target due to a damaged torpedo director, so the cruiser *Reno* finished the job off.

'There was great explosion and a huge mushroom-shaped cloud rose up over a thousand feet, and when the air cleared enough for us to try and figure out where the carrier might be located, the *Princeton* was gone. By this time it was 6.00 pm, and the longest day of my life was coming to a close.'

Like Paul Drury, Carl Brown, Jr, also lived a lifetime of aviation adventure in the course of this one mission. Slightly wounded, and flying a badly-damaged aeroplane, he experienced an epic of carrier flying;

'I don't know exactly how long the fight lasted. It was a long one – my guess is three to five minutes. I finished the fight with four Zekes on my tail arguing about who'd kill me. I used my last ditch manoeuvre: shove the stick forward as hard as I can with the throttle two-blocked and pitch full low. Nobody can follow that and shoot, so you gain at least a few seconds to think. As soon as I was headed straight down, I put the stick hard to the right for a spiral because the Zero couldn't turn well to the right at high speed. I lost them.

'*Princeton* was hit and the "Lex" and *Langley* refused to take me aboard because I had too much damage and might foul their deck. My instrument panel was well shot up, one fuel line in the cockpit was cut, and I had two to four inches of gas in the bottom of the bird. My port elevator hardly existed, and my tailhook was jammed, and I couldn't get it out with my emergency extension.

'I had two small shrapnel wounds in my left leg, but that was minor. I asked "Hatchet" (*Princeton*), who was still on the air although hit and burning, to tell the lead destroyer that I was going to ditch in front of him and to please pick me up.

One of the most dramatic photographs of a Hellcat ever taken, this 24 October shot shows a wounded Lt Carl Brown, Jr, of VF-27 gingerly taxying battle-damaged (164 holes) F6F-5 *PAPER DOLL* forward on *Essex*'s deck, having just completed a landing without hydraulics. Brown's former 'home', the *Princeton* (visible in the original print), had been mortally wounded by a lone bomb dropped through its flightdeck by a single 'Judy' which VF-27 had failed to intercept – as detailed in the text, Brown's division had accounted for 21.5 of the 36 aircraft downed by the unit as they blunted the early-morning strike on TF-38. *PAPER DOLL* had destroyed five Zekes in what was to be its pilot's last aerial combat (*US Navy*)

Hatchet said he'd pass the word. At that time *Essex* came on the air and said, "Hatchet 31. If you'll land immediately, we'll take you". You can imagine my relief.

'I lowered my gear with the emergency bottle – had no hydraulics, so I wouldn't have flaps for landing, nor an airspeed indicator (shot out), or cowl flaps or hook. The *Essex* captain had compassion and guts. I made a "British" approach from 500 ft. The LSO held a "Roger" on me til I was at the ramp when he gave me a fast, a high dip, and a cut. I had tested my controls and couldn't get the stick all the way back. I took the cut and snapped the stick as far as it would go. My tail hit the ramp hard, knocked the hook out, and I caught the first wire.'

Despite appalling losses, the Japanese kept throwing airpower at TF-38. About the same time VF-27 was engaged off Luzon, *Essex* launched fighters to intercept another large raid. Though he had been cautioned against personal involvement, Cdr David McCampbell led the scramble with VF-15's last seven Hellcats. Already the Navy's leading ace, his experience was badly needed.

The fighter director put McCampbell and his wingman Lt(jg) Roy Rushing onto a raid estimated at 80 hostiles. Lighting a cigarette, McCampbell assessed the situation and went to work. Maintaining altitude, and picking his targets carefully, he began whittling down the huge aerial armada. By the time he disengaged 90 minutes later through a lack of ammunition and fuel, he had claimed nine confirmed (five Zeros, two 'Oscars' and two 'Hamps') and two probables (a Zero and an 'Oscar'). Rushing flamed six more (four Zeros, an 'Oscar' and a 'Hamp'), while other *Essex* pilots downed a further ten Zekes or 'Vals'.

Meanwhile, Task Force 38 had struck repeatedly at powerful Japanese surface units approaching the Philippines from the west. Strike co-ordinators concentrated their dive- and torpedo-bombers on the enemy battleships, sinking the 64,000-ton *Musashi* and damaging six other ships.

By sundown the Japanese were withdrawing westward and the US carrier groups remained largely untouched. Hellcats had claimed nearly 200 kills during the long, frantic, day, including 21 by the three CVE squadrons – primarily VF-60 aboard *Suwannee*. Most heavily engaged were VF-19 with 53 kills, and VF-15 with 43.

The next day, 25 October, was one of mixed fortunes for the US Navy. It started badly and worsened through the morning as the Japanese central force unexpectedly emerged into Leyte Gulf, threatening Gen Douglas MacArthur's amphibious shipping. The battleship-cruiser force had reversed helm during the night, with merely an escort-carrier group in its path. Against awesome odds, and helped by other CVE units, 'Taffy Three' fought off the assault, losing one 'baby flattop' to surface gunfire and another to the newly-formed *kamikaze* corps.

Whilst Carl Brown, Jr, was taken below deck to the sick bay for treatment, his Hellcat was quickly pushed towards the bow in order to allow VF-15 to land back aboard. Just nine VF-27 Hellcats were airborne when *Princeton* was bombed, the remaining 16 aircraft having landed aboard the carrier to refuel and rearm, their pilots thinking that they had seen off the attack. The surviving F6Fs were soon pressed into service with their new units, who quickly painted out the distinctive cowling decoration and thus restored the Hellcats to regulation fleet finish (*Tailhook*)

Safely back in the USA, three veterans of VF-27's brief, but bloody, combat deployment point out to the press photographer exactly where their former 'home' can now be found. The young pilot with his finger on the globe is Ens Paul Drury (six kills), who is flanked by Ensigns Hugh Lillie (left, five kills) and Bob Burnell (right, four kills). The location for this shot is Drury's home at Ardmore, in Pennsylvania (*Bob Burnell via Mark Styling*)

Meanwhile, Adm W F Halsey steamed north in response to reports of Japanese carriers off the north-eastern tip of Luzon. His aviators found Vice Adm Ozawa's sacrificial four carriers and immediately went to work. The small, but spirited Japanese CAP, which numbered no more than 25 Zekes, was quickly swept aside as VF-15 splashed nine defenders. Four fell to Lt J R Strane, who ran his score to an even dozen – he scored his final kill (an 'Oscar') over Luzon on 5 November.

As McCampbell assigned targets from his lofty vantage point, a light carrier was damaged and a destroyer was sunk. He was then relieved as strike co-ordinator by Cdr Winters, who directed his own *Lexington* aircraft and other air groups against the survivors. By the time Winters departed, all three enemy flattops had been sunk or were sinking, including *Zuikaku*, the last of the Pearl Harbor attackers.

The Battle of Leyte Gulf effectively neutralised Japan's once powerful fleet. In four days between 23 and 26 October, the Imperial Navy lost 24 warships, including four carriers, three battleships and nine cruisers, and although submarines and surface combatants accounted for some of the Japanese losses, the huge majority succumbed to carrier airpower. Navy pilots and aircrews claimed 657 enemy aircraft shot down in exchange for 140 of their own number lost to all causes.

Liberation of the Philippines was no longer in doubt, if ever it had been, but the emergence of the *kamikaze* was an unsettling event. It would occupy the full attention of Hellcat pilots and fighter directors for the remaining ten months of the war.

## THE LONG HAUL

Japanese airpower in the Philippines, severely crippled at Leyte Gulf, lingered another two weeks. On 29 October fighter sweeps to Manila and fleet CAPs netted nearly 70 kills by Hellcat squadrons, including 38 by VF-18. Six days later VF-80 marked its debut as Lt Cdr Albert Vorse, Jr's (11.5 in total) *Ticonderoga* pilots notched their first dozen kills. Day-long combats over and around Clark Field accounted for 97 total victories. Thereafter, aerial encounters with Japanese aircraft dwindled to virtually nothing by early January.

That same day resulted in the loss of an outstanding FitRon as a suicidal Zero pilot boresighted *Lexington* and impacted near her island. She withdrew for repairs, prematurely ending VF-19's highly-successful cruise, accomplished without the loss of a bomber or 'torpecker' to enemy fighters. The 'Kittens" 155 victories ranked them eighth among all F6F squadrons in the number of kills scored on a single deployment.

Despite losing the services of experienced squadrons and air groups, the task force possessed a

Cdr McCampbell's nine-kill haul partially offset the news of the loss of *Princeton* that same morning for the 'folks back home'. *Minsi III* (BuNo 70143) was quickly polished up and decorated with 30 flags, and its pilot photographed in various poses for the national papers (*Tailhook*)

Pilots from VF-18 aboard *Intrepid* mill around the tail of a replacement F6F-3 prior to manning their Hellcats and heading off to strike Clark Field for the second time that day – 29 October 1944. A dozen enemy fighters had been downed on the first mission, and the unit went on to double that score in the afternoon sweep (*Jerry Scutts*)

depth of talent. As mentioned earlier, a perfect example of this was VF-18's Cecil Harris, who had splashed two floatplanes on 24 October, and logged his third 'quadruple' on the 29th. He added a lone Zero on 19 November, then downed four more enemy fighters on the 25th, running his wartime total to 23. With four quadruple kills, Harris was arguably the most consistently exceptional fighter pilot in the US Navy. He made maximum use of each opportunity, and only the battle damage sus-

tained by *Intrepid* prevented him from challenging McCampbell's spot as 'topgun.'

Another stand-out was VF-20's Ens Douglas Baker, a 23-year-old Oklahoman who demonstrated exceptional ability from the start. He flamed four fighters in his first combat on 12 October, and had run his tally to an even dozen by 14 November – the highest score ever attained by an ensign. That same day Cdr McCampbell destroyed one 'Oscar' and damaged another over Manila Bay, thus ending not only his own kill tally, but VF-15's as well.

By mid-November the most experienced Hellcat squadrons were finishing their tours, or were already en route home. These included several units which had been in almost constant combat since the Marianas campaign or before – VF-8, -14, -15 and -28, plus VF-27, which had been orphaned since the loss of *Princeton* the previous month.

'Fabled Fifteen' had recorded an eye-watering record since May. Through a combination of training, leadership and unprecedented opportunity, not only the fighter squadron but the entire air group had achieved extraordinary success at the 'Turkey Shoot', in the Philippines and beyond. Lt Cdr James F Rigg's unit (the latter had succeeded Cdr Brewer who was killed at Saipan) had scored 310 aerial victories and produced 26 aces, one of whom was his CAG, David McCampbell – the lat-

Wearing a white 13 on its fuselage and tail, this VF(N)-41 F6F-5N (seen being attached to the waist catapult on *Independence* in October 1944) was the mount of leading Navy nightfighter ace Lt William E Henry, who scored 9.5 kills between September 1944 and January 1945. His unit claimed a total of 46 kills whilst in the frontline, producing two aces in the process (*Tailhook*)

ter was now unassailable as the Navy's top ace with 34 victories. Later McCampbell was awarded the Medal of Honour for his spectacular success, thus becoming the only F6F pilot accorded that distinction, and the only carrier aviator so honoured in the last three years of the war.

While many top scorers rotated home, other aces were returning for a second and even third tour. One such pilot was Lt Alex Vraciu, formerly of VFs -6 and then -16. Though recently married, Vraciu

Another ace's aircraft, F6F-5 'Ginger 29' was the occasional mount of VF-11's Lt Jim Swope, who claimed five kills whilst flying Hellcats from *Hornet*. Like his great friend Charlie Stimpson, Swope had been land-based with the 'Sundowners' in Guadalcanal in 1943, where he claimed 4.666 kills whilst flying the Wildcat – his combined score placed him second in VF-11's aces listing behind Stimpson (*Jerry Scutts*)

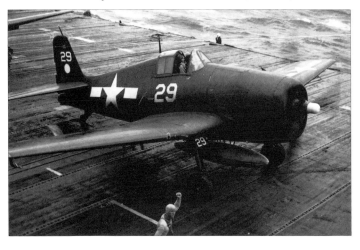

VF-15 pipped VF-18 to the title of 'Topguns' for the Leyte action by a mere 1.5 kills – 140.5 versus 139! This group shot of 'Fighting Fifteen' was taken days before they were replaced on *Essex* by VF-4 on 17 November. VF-15 produced 26 aces during its seven months at sea. The backdrop for this photo is provided by *Minsi III* (F6F-5 BuNo 70143)

Armed up with four 5-in rockets apiece, VF-15 F6Fs are marshalled forward past the waist hangar lift on *Essex* prior to launching for a strike on shipping in Subic Bay on 5 November. Seven aircraft were downed during the sweep, including kills 31 and 32 to Cdr McCampbell in *Minsi III*. Aside from the CAG's success, the remaining victories were shared by five VF-15 aces (*Jerry Scutts*)

was anxious to return to combat, and when he reported to *Lexington* in November, the ship was still recovering from *kamikaze* damage and preparing to bid farewell to Air Group 19. Vraciu remained aboard just briefly, before joining VF-20 in *Enterprise*. There was a fitting symmetry to this assignment, as Vraciu's friend and mentor, 'Butch' O'Hare, had been the 'Big E's' CAG when he was lost off Tarawa in 1943.

However, on 14 December Vraciu was shot down while flying his second mission with 'Fighting Twenty', Japanese AA gunners succeeding where 19 of their aviators had failed. He bailed out of F6F-5 BuNo 58831 near Bamban Airfield, and was quickly scooped up by friendly Filipino USAFFE guerillas. He remained on the ground, gathering information on the Japanese defences around Clark Field for a further six weeks, before returning to US control. Despite eventually making it back to his carrier, Vraciu was soon sent back to America as the Navy policy at the time dictated that servicemen who had spent time behind enemy lines were not allowed to return to combat for fear of capture.

The 14th was a bad day for Hellcat aces generally, as Vraciu's squadron-mate, the recently-promoted Lt(jg) Douglas Baker, went missing soon after he had destroyed three Zekes and an 'Oscar' – Vraciu was eventually given Baker's dogtags as proof of death. With 16 victories to his credit, the latter was well on his way to the upper ranks of the Navy aces. That same day five-kill VF-29 ace Lt(jg) W D Bishop bailed out of his F6F following a mid-air collision over Subic Bay. He was seen on the ground the next day, but mysteriously disappeared before he could be rescued.

On a more positive note, Lt R H

Anderson (8.5 in total) of VF-80 became the 28th, and last, Hellcat instant ace of 1944 on this date. His unit, nicknamed 'Vorse's Vipers', tangled with a mixed formation of Zekes and 'Oscars' over the Philippines, and Anderson claimed five in as many minutes. The potent team of Lts Patrick D Fleming (19 in total) and Richard L Cormier (eight in total) added four apiece en route to acedom, while their *Ticonderoga* squadronmates accounted for ten more. It was the realisation of a dream for 'Zeke' Cormier, who had previously flown Avengers on mundane anti-submarine patrols in the Atlantic.

---

**Occupation of Leyte** – *10 October to 30 November 1944*

| | | |
|---|---|---|
| VF-15 | *Essex* | 140.50 |
| VF-18 | *Intrepid* | 139 |
| VF-20 | *Enterprise* | 135.16 |
| VF-19 | *Lexington* | 127 |
| VF-14 | *Wasp* | 87.50 |
| VF-11 | *Hornet* | 82 |
| VF-8 | *Bunker Hill* | 74 |
| VF-29 | *Cabot* | 72 |
| VF-13 | *Franklin* | 67.50 |
| VF-27 | *Princeton* | 59 |

Total by 22 F6F squadrons – 1300.16

---

**Top Hellcat Pilots of the Leyte Occupation**

| | | | |
|---|---|---|---|
| Lt C E Harris | VF-18 | 18 | Total 23 |
| Cdr D McCampbell | CVG-15 | 15 | Total 34 |
| Ens D Baker | VF-20 | 12.33 | Total 16.33 |
| Lt W J Masoner | VF-19 | 10 | Total 12 |
| Lt C R Stimpson | VF-11 | 10 | Total 16 |

VF-80 was one of a number of newly-formed squadrons to make its combat debut over Luzon in November 1944. Flying from USS *Ticonderoga*, the 'Vipers' enjoyed considerable success during their solitary frontline deployment, having claimed 159.5 kills by the time they returned to the US on 1 April 1945. This shot was taken on 5 November – the date on which VF-80 claimed its first six kills – as the Hellcats are lined up for launch. Half of the day's victory tally fell to future aces (*Tailhook*)

In response to the increasing suicide threat, big-deck air groups experienced a profound change shortly before year's end. Fighter complements were raised from 54 to 73 Hellcats – the fourth increase since June 1942 – with Marine Corps F4U units also helping to fill the gap. *Essex* was the first to embark one of these composite air groups, as two Corsair squadrons augmented Lt Cdr K G Hammond's (two kills in total) VF-4 in December.

The increase in fighters meant that fewer SB2Cs and TBMs could be embarked, and normally the VB and VT squadrons were reduced to 15 aircraft apiece. However, as a

This panoramic view, taken from *Ticonderoga*'s bridge, shows TF-38 *Essex*-class carriers (from left to right) *Wasp*, *Hornet*, *Hancock* and *Yorktown* at anchor of Ulithi Atoll on 2 December 1944. The original caption for this shot read 'Murderer's Row'! Each carrier boasted an air group of 100 aircraft, approximately half of which were Hellcats assigned at that stage to one almost unwieldy (at least administratively) squadron

Three of VF-11's most successful pilots recount their experiences in the wardroom pantry following the 'Sundowners'' awesome display of aerial supremacy in the environs of Clark Field on 5 November. Jim Swope (left) and Blake 'Rabbit' Moranville (right) both scored kills on the early-morning Strike Able, sharing four 'Tojos', plus a 'Betty' for the latter. 'Charlie' Stimpson's two 'Oscars' and a 'Tojo' were claimed two hours later during the follow-up Strike Baker sweep

VF-11's 'Ginger 13' prepares to be loaded with two 500-lb bombs in readiness for a strike on Tan Son Nhut airport in French Indochina. F6Fs could carry two bombs beneath the wings, but a single 500-pounder was the most frequent option. A standard techniques was to letdown from 15,000 ft in a 50-degree descent, releasing at 3500 ft. Skip-bombing was also performed by Hellcat units against thin-skinned ships. Flying low, pilots released their ordnance in level flight and pulled up over the target as the delayed-action bomb skipped off the water and penetrated the ship's hull

temporary measure *Essex* and *Wasp* 'beached' their Helldivers and operated 91 fighters with 15 Avengers.

## INDOCHINA INTERLUDE

The fast carriers bade farewell to the Philippines on 10 January 1945 when VF(N)-41 splashed four bandits. The first major operation of the new year was an anti-shipping sweep of the East China Sea, where no Allied warships had steamed in three years. Though intelligence indicated significant Japanese fleet units along the Indochina coast, none turned up. Fighter sweeps and CAPs of 12 January netted 14 shootdowns for Hellcat squadrons, including 11 by VF-3. It was a significant boost, as Lt Cdr W L Lamberson's (three kills in total) pilots had claimed just eight kills aboard *Yorktown* since October. Near Saigon a 'Tony' and a 'Hamp' fell to Lt John L Schell (five kills in total), who was destined to become one of only two F6F aces produced by the squadron – Lt(jg) James M Jones was the other pilot, and he scored two of his eventual seven kills with VF-3. He eventually attained ace status with VBF-3 (the only pilot to do so) following reassignment to the latter unit after VF-3 had split in two on 1 February 1945.

As usual, F6F squadrons flew the huge majority of missions on the 12th, Hellcats logging 1065 of the task force's 1457 combat sorties, or nearly three-quarters of the total. Twenty-one carrier aircraft were lost in the process.

Among the dozen F6F pilots shot down was Lt(jg) Blake Moranville, a VF-11 ace with six kills. The engine of his F6F-5 BuNo 70680 was holed by flak while strafing Tan Son Nhut, and he was forced to belly-land in a rice paddy. Captured by the Vichy French, he and five other downed fliers were moved to a compound near Hanoi just prior to open hostilities erupting between the French and Japanese. Moranville then embarked on an epic adventure capped by an overland march to Dien Bien Phu with a Foreign Legion unit. Eventually

flown to Kunming, in China, he safely returned to the US. There he resumed his duties as keeper of 'Gunner', VF-11's Boston Terrier mascot.

Moranville was one of only two Navy aces known to have been taken prisoner in the Pacific War, the other being VF-15's 20-year-old Ens Kenneth A Flinn (five kills in total), who was shot down near Nansei Shoto on 13 October 1944. He survived more than nine months of captivity only to die of malnutrition three weeks before Japan capitulated.

By January 1945 the new 73-plane/110-pilot organisation of *Essex*-class FitRons was recognised as being administratively unmanageable. Therefore, Commander Naval Air Forces Pacific authorised air groups to divide their fighter-force into two squadrons. Generally, the existing CO retained the VF organisation, while his executive officer – normally another lieutenant commander – formed a fighter-bomber unit, designated VBF. Maintenance remained as before, with both squadrons flying the same aircraft. However, some air groups later deployed with mixed complements of Hellcat fighters and Corsair fighter-bombers.

The VF/VBF split was described in the following terms by Lt Cdr Marshall Beebe (10.5 kills), commanding officer of the reformed VF-17;

'The fact that the F6F was equipped with wing bomb racks and a centreline rack made it doubly useful as a fighter-bomber. During training at NAS Alameda, California, the squadron was increased from 36 to 54 aeroplanes. Then during the short period in Hawaii the complement was increased to 72 aircraft with 102 pilots.

'The aircraft and pilots were transferred from VF-6, which fortunately had received some inter-squadron tactical training on the west coast. In January 1945, while at Guam, the squadron was divided into two 36-aircraft squadrons – VF and VBF – for administrative purposes. The two squadrons flew almost identical operations.'

The first ace of the new year was Lt C M Craig, VF-22's acting CO aboard *Cowpens*. On 21 January he led his division into a formation of *kamikazes* off Formosa and returned to 'Mighty Moo' with five confirmed 'Tojos', for a wartime total of 11.75 kills.

That month Cdr T F Caldwell's Night Air Group 41 completed its deployment aboard *Independence*. Though slow to gain acceptance, the night-flying Hellcats and Avengers eventually proved the validity of the

Packed into VF-11's ready-room deep in the bowels of *Hornet*, pilots on the Indochina strike make notes on their flight maps prior to walking to their aircraft. The pilot with 'Gunner' (the squadron mascot) on his lap is Lt(jg) Bill Eccles (four kills), whilst to his left is Lt Jimmie 'Doc' Savage (seven kills)

As mentioned earlier, Lt William E Henry of VF(N)-41 was the leading Navy nightfighter ace of the war, with six of his 9.5 kills being scored in full or semi-darkness. He later led F4U-5N Corsair nightfighter-equipped VC-3 Det C on USS *Valley Forge* during the first year of the Korean War (*Barrett Tillman*)

Smaller CVL-based F6F units contributed a great deal to the overall victory in the Pacific. One such outfit was VF-22 aboard USS *Cowpens*, whose 24 pilots downed 50 aircraft between 13 September 1944 and 21 January 1945. This shot was taken just prior to the unit being relieved, and shows VF-22's 'Sockeye 7' division which comprised; Ens Ben C Amsden (standing, far left) with five kills; Lt(jg) Bob A Richardson (standing, middle) with 3.25 kills; Ens Mike J Roche (standing, right) with 3.5 kills; Ens Arthur 'Ike' DeSellier (front row, left), 0.25 of a kill; and Lt(jg) Joe A Degutis, also with a quarter-kill (*Ben Amsden via Mark Styling*)

This VMF(N)-541 'Bat Eyes' F6F-5N was photographed at Peleliu prior to the squadron heading north to the Philippines (*Tailhook*)

dedicated nocturnal air group, both in offensive and defensive measures. VF(N)-41 closed its account with an 'Oscar' splashed off Canton on 16 January – the squadron's 46th confirmed kill. It was also the tenth victory for former SBD pilot Lt William E Henry, who was one of the unit's two aces. The other was Ens Jack S Berkheimer, who had scored to 7.5 kills before disappearing during a mission over Luzon the previous month.

Bill Henry's combat was not limited to night interceptions, however, as VF(N)-41 also engaged in nocturnal strike and heckler missions. Ironically, in some ways the most trying experience for the aircrew of the 'Indy' was not the stress of a night combat, but having to play the passive role of spectator on the deck during daylight *kamikaze* raids, as Henry explained;

'A few days out of the China Sea the day fighters were hitting Formosa and we did CAP or standby all night until the second day, then suicide planes came out by the dozens. Therefore, it was decided to put some of us VFN up to help.

'I was sitting in my plane, turning up, parked in the landing area when I saw everyone get off the flightdeck. I soon saw why. A 'Judy' was heading for us from the port quarter. All I could do was sit and look. As he flew over the battleship next to us, they got him and he rolled over on his back and crashed in our wake. They decided not to launch me.

'Later in the afternoon they decided to try to put some of us up again. This time I was in the plane on the port catapult. I was not turning up. Here came a Zero heading for us. He had trouble pushing over to hit us, and was going to overshoot, so he flattened out and flew into the side of a CVL right next to us, probably *Langley*. He burst into flames but most of the plane fell into the water and the fire went out. Again they cancelled the launch. About 30 minutes later I saw a CV burning in formation off our starboard bow. It was the *Ticonderoga* (143 killed and 202 wounded).'

Relieving CVLG(N)-41 was the fleet's first big-deck 'night owl' unit, Air Group 90 aboard *Enterprise*. The CAG was Cdr William I Martin, a veteran SBD and TBF pilot who had pioneered the night attack role for torpedo- and dive-bomber units in US naval aviation. With 30 F6F-5Ns and -5Es (plus two photo-birds), VF(N)-90 was led by Lt Cdr R J McCullough, whose pilots would shortly be introduced to combat.

About this same time, Marine Corps night Hellcats were carving a reputation for themselves in the Philippines. Lt Col Peter Lambrecht's VMF(N)-541 arrived at Tacloban Airfield in December and, in barely a month, shot down 23 enemy aircraft that had proved too fast for USAAF P-61 Black Widows to engage. Ironically, most of the kills were scored in daylight, as the initial night kills evidently dissuaded Japanese fighter-bombers from snooping around. The top shooters were 1st Lt Harold T Hayes and Tech Sgt John W Andre, each with four kills. Later commissioned, Andre became an ace with another nightfighter victory (this time in an F4U-5N Corsair of VMF(N)-513) seven years later, in Korea (see *Aces 4 Korean War Aces* by Robert F Dorr, Jon Lake and Warren Thompson).

# TOKYO BOUND

The new organisation in Task Force 38 had just been implemented when the fast carriers attacked Tokyo. With barely time to 'shake out' the VF/VBF split and absorb the new night fliers, 16 fast carriers aimed their bows at the Japanese homeland for two days of strikes in mid-February.

A predawn launch on the 16th kicked off a day-long series of combats over and around the Japanese capital. Strenuous opposition, combined with poor weather – as low as 1000-ft ceilings – conspired to produce a major challenge for the relatively inexperienced carrier pilots. In fact, for seven of the embarked air groups, the Tokyo strikes were their introduction to combat.

Other than two roving 'Betty' bombers splashed by the CAP, the first overland combat was found by VF-9, now riding *Lexington* on their third deployment in less than two-and-a-half years. Over Katori, Lt Cdr Herbert N Houck's (six kills in total) pilots found a mixture of Zekes and 'Nates', claiming 12 confirmed and four probables. This was just the beginning, as 'Fighting Nine' logged eight more victories during the day.

However, the *Lexington* Hellcats paid a price for their success. One pilot failed to appear at the rendezvous after the first sweep, and two more were lost on the second – apparently the victims of Japanese fighters. One was the CAG, Cdr Phil Torrey, Jr, (two kills in total) who had led VF-9 during the 1943-44 cruise. He was last seen making a head-on pass at a 'Tojo', but was then lost to sight during the erratic manoeuvres.

Ens Wiliam G Bailey, USNR, of VF-33 was lucky to step from the wreckage of his F6F without a scratch following this rather dramatic landing back aboard USS *Sangamon* on 26 February 1945. The small confines of the escort carrier greatly reduced the pilots' margin for error when landing back aboard. Bailey's predicament was caused by a 'floating' landing, which saw him catch a wire too late to avoid hitting the island (*Philip Jarrett*)

Most heavily engaged was VF-80, which found repeated opportunities in the Katori and Imba areas. The 'Vipers' claimed two-dozen victims in the morning, paced by Lt Cdr L W Keith (5.5 kills in total) with five, while their original CO, *Hancock's* CAG, Lt Cdr 'Scoop' Vorse, Jr, led other divisions to 13 more victories over Chiba Peninsula. During the fight Vorse gained four victories, running his wartime total to 11.5. Only one Hellcat was hit by enemy gunfire.

VF-80 fought four more combats during the day, including a dogfight over Imba Airfield that saw Lt A L Anderson (5.5 kills in total) destroy five fighters representing four different types – two 'Oscars', a Zeke, a 'Tojo' and a 'Tony'. In the same area Lt W C Edwards, Jr (7.5 kills in total), also emerged as an instant ace, downing two 'Nates', two Zekes and an 'Oscar'.

Then, shortly past noon, five pilots intercepted more Zekes and 'Oscars' between Imba and Mobara Airfields. Lt Pat Fleming shot down five of the former, while his section leader, 'Zeke' Cormier, got three more. Other 'Vipers' claimed seven additional kills. Then, late that afternoon, three pilots claimed four more victories for a squadron total of 71 confirmed and 15 probables throughout the day. It was a record unsurpassed in American aviation, made possible by the fact that CVG-80 did not distinguish between VF and VBF units.

The day's top personal scores included five by Cdr Gordon Schecter (five kills in total), skipper of VF-45. He gunned three Zekes and shared two other kills in the morning (a 'Dinah' and an ancient 'Claude'), then added an 'Oscar' late that afternoon. Ens R R Kidwell, Jr, also claimed five kills in two missions, these being his only scores of the war. In fact, the *San Jacinto* squadron made an extremely-impressive showing with 28 kills, second only to VF-80's record tally. Though every fighter squadron in the task force achieved kills, most of the CVL units had to be content with flying ForceCAP patrols over the carriers.

This operation marked the first time that F4Us were embarked in strength, as *Bunker Hill's* air group included not only VF-84, but two Marine Corsair outfits also, while *Essex* too boasted a pair of 'Leatherneck' squadrons. In all, the F4Us accounted for 27 of the day's total of 291 aerial claims.

Although 17 January had brought significant combat, it was clear that Japanese airpower had taken a beating the day before. Another 97 shoot-downs were claimed as 11 Hellcat squadrons accounted for all but 29 of the total. Leading the pack was *Yorktown's* VBF-3, adding 13 victories to the previous day's 23. In fact, the two-day Tokyo strike represented the fighter-bomber outfit's only aerial claims of the deployment.

*Wasp's* VF-81 claimed 11 kills on the 17th and also crowned its sole ace – on the 16th and 17th Lt(jg) H V Sherrill added 4.5 victories to his one previous credit. *Essex's* 'Fighting Four' counted 22 shootdowns during the operation, of which three went to Lt D E Laird, running his Pacific War tally to five. Combined with his two shared Luftwaffe kills (0.5 of a Ju 88 and 0.25 of a He 115) from *Ranger's* 1943 Norway strike, 'Diz' Laird became the only Navy ace with confirmed victories against both Germany and Japan although indisputably a five-kill ace, Hollis Hills of VF-32 is technically not a US Navy ace as his first kill was scored against the Luftwaffe whilst he was part of the Royal Canadian Air Force.

Back in a big way was VF-80, as Pat Fleming continued to add to his burgeoning tally. He took three divisions on a sweep south-west of Katori airfield, stirring up 'Nates', 'Oscars', Zekes and 'Tojos' in the process.

Fire is the thing most feared on a carrier, and the Hellcat's ability to set itself alight was further 'fuelled' by the gas stored in its external tank, which invariably ruptured if the aircraft suffered a heavy landing. This VF-9 F6F-5 had its belly tank ripped off by the arrestor wires as it landed back aboard *Lexington* on 25 February 1945, the pilot running down the wing and jumping to safety. Note how the fabric-covered elevators have already burnt through and that the prop is still turning

Two-tour veteran Jim Swope scored his fifth, and last, F6F kill on 15 January 1945. His 'Jill' was one of six victories credited to the 'Sundowners' on this day as they patrolled off the coast of Hong Kong. Tour-expired, he returned to the US in February 1945 (*Tailhook*)

The *Hancock* pilots shot down 12, of which Fleming claimed four. He had downed nine Japanese aircraft in well under 24 hours, running his score to 19. He remained tied as the Navy's fourth-ranked fighter ace for the rest of the war. Moreover, the 'Vipers' were credited with 83 kills during the Tokyo strikes – more than one-quarter of the two-day total. In all, TF-38 lost 88 aircraft, including 28 to operational accidents and poor weather.

The fast carriers were back off Japan on 18 March, launching far-ranging sweeps of airfields and searching for enemy warships. *Hornet's* VF-17 found repeated combat around Kanoya as CO, Lt Cdr Marshall Beebe, and Lt Robert C Coats (9.333 kills in total) each claimed five victories. Formerly CO of VC-39, Beebe had swum away from the torpedoed escort carrier *Liscombe Bay* in 1943, but was now well on his way to double ace status. Bob Coats, who later admitted to being the only non-swimming ace

in Navy history, downed five Zekes. In all, the squadron claimed 32 victories that morning.

The next day *Essex's* new VF-83 logged its first nine kills. Its VBF 'twin' squadron, flying F4Us, had already been blooded the day before, and both outfits would be heard from repeatedly in the ensuing five months.

That same morning, approaching Kure Naval Base, *Hornet* Hellcats were intercepted by a small force of enemy fighters flown both competently and aggressively, which effectively tied up the strike escort. One of the pilots was Lt Robert A Clark (six kills in total), who quickly downed a 'George' and a Zeke early in the fight. By that point, 'the radio was a scrambled jabber of pilots screeching for help and yelling advice. I noticed about 3000 ft above us a circle of Jap planes apparently loafing through the fight, but I soon saw their game. They'd formed a "Lufbery" circle, World War 1 style, and were waiting until a Hellcat got on some Jap's tail. Then they'd jump him in section and shoot him down, and return to the upper circle. This tactic worked as one Hellcat went screaming by me in a plunging dive with his belly tank on fire. Someone was yelling on the radio, "Drop it! For God's sake, drop it – you're on fire!" The sky was a flaming kaleidoscope of burning aeroplanes, flashing insignia and lancing tracer. Four or five chutes floated gently downward.

'After getting back to the *Hornet*, we rendezvoused the survivors of out ill-fated sweep. We had lost eight. We had accounted for 25 Japanese aircraft, and also discoverd that our dive-bombers and torpedo aircraft had

VF-17 was one of the most successful units involved in the final carrier push into Japanese home waters in 1945, scoring 161 kills between February and May. Its primary weapon throughout this period was the F6F-5 Hellcat (72 machines split between VF- and VBF-17), although as this shot clearly shows, a handful of late-build -3s also saw service into the Okinawan campaign – indeed, 'White 41' was probably one of the last of its type in TF-58. Twelve pilots achieved ace status on this deployment with VF-17, plus a further eight with 'twin' unit VBF-17 (*Jerry Scutts*)

Texan Lt(jg) Tilman E Poole was one of VF-17 aces on its Hellcat deployment, claiming six kills and one probable during roving sweeps of southern Japan between 18 March and 12 April. He had earlier seen combat in F6F-3s as a replacement pilot with VF-39 in the Marshalls, dive-bombing pockets of Japanese resistance on bypassed islands in the region
(*Tilman Pool via Mark Styling*)

The outstanding fighter squadron of the Okinawan invasion in terms of aerial kills was VF-83 aboard *Essex*. Between 1 April and 23 June its pilots downed 122 aircraft, whilst naval aviators of the 'twinned' VBF-83 claimed a further 60. Both units used identically-marked F6F-5s, the carrier embarking 70+ Hellcats decorated with Air Group 83's 'hour glass' motif on the fin and upper wing surfaces. This 19 April shot shows Hellcats being marshalled into position prior to launching against the island of Ie Shima, off the west coast of Okinawa

had excellent success at the Kure base with minimum losses', Clark later related.

Two days later VBF-17 again led the *Hornet* hit parade. Lt(jg) Henry E Mitchell (six kills in total) led an interception offshore which resulted in eight kills – five 'Bettys' by Mitchell and two 'Bettys' and a Zero shared by his division.

## ORDEAL OFF OKINAWA

Operation *Iceburg*, the invasion of Okinawa, began on Easter Sunday, 1 April 1945. Officially, it lasted 83 days until 23 June, and in that period carrier-based F6Fs splashed on average ten enemy aircraft a day.

In 12 weeks the embarked Hellcat squadrons claimed 837 shootdowns, led by *Essex's* VF-83 (122 kills) and *Yorktown's* VF-9 (93), while the F6Fs of VBF-9 added 44 more. In fact, 'Fighting Nine' was so heavily engaged that it produced the top three scorers of the campaign. Lt Eugene A Valencia was already a seven-kill ace when he took his division into combat as a thoroughly well-drilled team. During 'turn-around' training at NAS Pasco, Washington, Gene Valencia had bribed sailors with alcohol in exchange for more fuel, thus allowing additional flight time. His methods may have been unorthodox, but the results would speak for themselves.

The fourth-heaviest day of air combat in the carrier war occurred on 6 April, resulting in 257 Navy victories. The stats for this day came as no surprise to fighter pilots and radar controllers, who counted ten major raids during the afternoon. Some 355 *kamikazes* and 340 bomber or escort aircraft were flung at the task force, not all of which found their targets. Still, there were enough to keep all hands busy past sunset. *Belleau Wood's* VF-30 accounted for 47, and three ensigns claimed 16.5 kills among them – C C Foster got six (8.5 kills in total), K J Dahms 5.5 (seven kills in total), and J G Miller (eight kills in total) bagged five. That same day VF-17 splashed 25 as Lt(jg) W E Hardy (6.5 kills in total) ran his score from zero to five in 70 frenetic minutes, returning to *Hornet* at dark – VBF-17 added 21 more.

The major beneficiaries of this intense activity were Cdr J J Southerland II's VF-83 pilots, as *Essex's* Hellcats splashed 56 raiders in six combats around the Ryukyus. The CO bagged two 'Tonys' en route to scoring five kills exactly – a long way from his VF-5 days over Guadalcanal where he had duelled with Saburo Sakai in early August 1942 – Southerland scored his final kill (a Zeke) on 29 April whilst serving as CO of VF-23 aboard *Langley*. Three other pilots claimed four kills each – Lt(jg)s H N Batten and S J Brocato (both scored seven in total), plus Ens J M Barnes (six kills in total) – they all made ace on this day.

Despite the tireless efforts of the F6F and F4U pilots, enough attackers penetrated the CAP to hit 19 ships, sinking six. No carriers were damaged, but radar picket destroyers sustained heavy damage with ten hit and three sunk.

On 7 April TF-38 intercepted a very different type of suicide mission. Japan's greatest remaining battleship, the 64,000-ton *Yamato*, was found off the south-west coast of Kyushu, en route to Okinawa with her screen of nine escorts. Unopposed from the air, the task force sent day-long strikes of dive- and torped-bombers under lowering skies against the dreadnaught, and although AA gunners downed nine carrier aircraft (including two F6Fs), *Yamato*, a light cruiser and four destroyers were sunk.

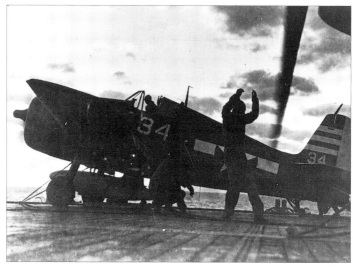

During the day Hellcats splashed 32 bandits, although one put a bomb into *Hancock*, before following the ordnance through the flightdeck. Badly damaged, the ship and Air Group Six were forced out of action until early June. 'Fighting Six' had claimed 15 kills since arriving in March, but the two-month enforced lay-off prevented the veteran squadron from producing any further aces.

During interceptions on the 12th, VF-31 ace Michele Mazzocco (five kills in total) tangled with a well-flown 'Tojo' near Okinawa, and learned just how rugged the F6F really was. Although the *Belleau Wood* pilot inflicted early damage on the Nakajima, its pilot continued the fight. After chasing tails downward from 18,000 ft, Mazzocco and the Japanese flier approached one another head on. Both began firing, and both scored hits. Then the New Yorker realised, 'he wasn't going to veer off, and a collision was not only inevitable, but planned by him.

'I waited until the last possible moment, my heart in my throat, then pulled up hard and to the right. His left wing came through the bottom arc of my prop and debris flew all over the sky. The concussion was tremendous, and jarred me to the bone, and I lost control of my plane for a moment that seemed an eternity.

'When I recovered, I could see him spinning slowly down toward the sea. My wingman checked my plane and told me my belly tank had taken most of the punishment in the collision. I managed to jettison it and made an emergency landing on the carrier. "Mr Grumman" surely built a tough one when he built that Hellcat. God bless him.'

On 16 April the *kamikazes* tried hard again, but failed to match the strength of their efforts ten days earlier. VF-17's Lt(jg) J T 'Stump' Crosby nevertheless capitalised upon a long-awaited opportunity. Having completed a previous deployment with VF-18 in 1943/44, during which he had claimed a quarter-kill of a 'Betty', Crosby had further damaged two fighters on this tour and was ready for 'acedom'. That morning he chased down three 'Jacks', a Zero and a 'Val' to become *Hornet's* tenth, and last, instant ace – a record for all carriers. TF-38 carrier pilots claimed 157 victories during the day, which was exactly 100 fewer than their total on 6 April.

Braced onto the forward catapult, a VF-29 F6F-5 is just seconds away from being shot off the bow of USS *Cabot* at the start of a dawn sweep along the Japanese coast in mid-February. The unit scored 113 kills and produced 12 aces during its seven-month stint in the Pacific

Joint second top-scorer in VF-29 was Ens Franklin 'Trooper' Troup, who downed seven aircraft between 15 October 1944 and 4 April 1945. His tally of 20 bomb markings alongside the kill symbols denotes that VF-29 could also carrying out the fighter-bomber role – a task that assumed greater importance as more and more Hellcats were thrust into the frontline
(*Franklin Troup via Mark Styling*)

'Valencia's Flying Circus' of VF-9 holds the record as being the high-est-scoring fighter division in Navy history. Lt Eugene Valencia's team was credited with 43.5 kills during their 1945 det. This shot shows from left; Lt(jg) H E Mitchell ten kills); Lt(jg) C L Smith (six kills); Lt(jg) J B French (11 kills); and Valencia, whose first tour score of 7.5 combined with his 15.5 in 1945 to make 50, all without the loss of a single Hellcat (*Barrett Tillman*)

Ens Donald M McPherson was just one of 12 pilots to score five or more kills with VF-83 during its 1945 deployment. His first aerial kills came on 6 April when he downed two 'Vals' near Kikai Jima, followed on 4 May by three 'Alf' biplanes that had been re-rolled from recce float-planes into *kamikaze* bombers – over 100 aircraft were downed in one frantic hour on this date as the Japanese launched a huge assault on TF-38 (*Donald McPherson*)

During the Okinawa campaign, 'Fighting Nine's' Gene Valencia added 12.5 victories to his own score while all three pilots in his division became aces. His section leader, Lt(jg) James B French (11 kills in total), and wingman Lt(jg) Harris E Mitchell (ten kills in total), both became double aces, whilst the number-four man in the team, Lt(jg) Clinton L Smith, shot down six Japanese aircraft.

The division's combat debut had occurred during the February Tokyo strikes, but their next taste of action could hardly have been more spectacular. Patrolling over a picket destroyer on 17 April, Valencia was vectored onto 'ten-plus' bogies which quickly grew into 25 Zekes and 'Franks'. Attacking from the 'perch', Valencia ignored the odds and led his three pilots into the swarm of Japanese, his first burst exploding the topmost 'Frank' and thus signalling the start of a ten-minute dogfight. During that time Harris Mitchell shot three Zekes off his leader's tail, allowing Valencia to concentrate on his own shooting.

When burning aeroplanes stopped falling into the sea, the team regrouped and circled the combat area. Valencia and company counted eight parachutes still in the air among the 17 kills claimed. 'Only' 14 were confirmed – six by Valencia, four by French, three by Mitchell and one by Smith. The only damage sustained by the F6Fs was superficial dents and scrapes caused by the debris of disintegrating enemy aircraft.

TF-38's next major action occured on 4 May when task force fighters splashed 105 bandits throughout the Ryukyus. The shooting started well before dawn as VF-9's nightfighter detachment dropped four snooping 'Bettys', three of which fell to Ens John Orth, taking took his final score to six. *Yorktown's* 'day shift' also contributed by claiming a further 29 kills, including 11 by Valencia's well-drilled team.

VF-83 splashed two-dozen suiciders near Izema Shima where, in his second and last combat, Ens Myron M Truax (seven kills in total) claimed four Type 93 trainers, a 'Val' and an 'Oscar'. By mid-morning the scoring was over, with VBF-12 and VF-46 bringing the day's Hellcat tally to 73 – *Essex, Bunker Hill* and the new *Shangri-La's* Corsairs added 30 more.

Come the dawn of 11 May, the task force's air defence had proven invincible for three full weeks, but that record sequence was tragically ended in a combined *kamikaze* and dive-bombing attack which knocked *Bunker Hill* out of the war. After controlling terrible fires, CV-17 limped away with some 650 casualties, including 389 dead. Elsewhere, VF-9 claimed 20 more kills and Lt Bert Eckard (seven kills in total) became the 46th, and last, Hellcat ace in a day when he splashed five Zekes north-east of Okinawa.

Despite appalling losses among their ranks, the suiciders kept coming. Their persistence ended *Enterprise's* superb career on 14 May, prematurely stopping Night Air Group 90's tour. The Night Hellcats of

Although officially frowned upon, nose art was worn very occasionally on Pacific theatre Hellcats, with this previously unknown example being one of the gaudiest. F6F-5 BuNo 72534 was christened *DEATH N' DESTRUCTION* by a trio of ensign aces serving with VF-83 in April 1945, the name being further embellished with a skull and cross-bones! Donald McPherson, Bill Kingston, Jr, and Lyttleton Ward each flew the fighter on numerous occasions over Okinawa, with the latter definitely shooting down three 'Alfs' and an 'Oscar' in it during the 4 May mass attack, and becoming an ace in the process (*Bill Kingston via Mark Styling*)

VF(N)-90 had claimed 31 shootdowns by this stage, including 4.5 by Lt Owen D Young (three 'Jakes', a 'Tony' and a shared 'Pete'), all of which were destroyed in an 83-minute spell on the morning of 12 May.

However, with repeated scoring opportunities came unrelenting operations, and the constant strain of CAPs, strike escorts and occasional close air support quickly used up squadrons and air groups; units deploying for an expected six-month tour were worn out in four.

In June VF-9 ended its second Pacific deployment, turning over to VF-88 in *Yorktown*. Against the loss of five pilots, the original Hellcat squadron had claimed 128.75 aerial victories and 47 on the ground during 1574 combat sorties. In compiling its record, VF-9 expended 543,600 rounds of .50 cal ammunition, over 300 bombs and 750 rockets. In all, 'Fighting Nine's' two F6F tours totalled 250.75 aerial kills (plus six Vichy aircraft during *Torch* in 1942). Thus, VF-9 became the Navy's second-ranked Hellcat squadron behind VF-15. 'Fighting Nine' produced 20 aces throughout the war, a tally only exceeded by VF-2 (27 aces) and VF-15 (26 aces). At war's end VF-9's Lt Gene Valencia was the Navy's second-ranking ace with 23 victories, being tied in this position with Lt Cecil Harris of VF-18.

Another notable achievement by a VF-9 pilot was the consistent record of Lt Marvin J Franger. Originally a 23-year-old ensign aboard *Ranger* for

Late in the afternoon on 3 April 1945, Lt(jg) Mel Cozzens was part of a VF-29 division that intercepted a small force of Zekes and 'Tonys' inbound to TF-38 south of Kikai Jima. Five pilots shared ten kills, Cozzens claiming the lion's share with two Zekes and a 'Tony' falling to BuNo 71972's guns – this almost doubled his score from 3.5 to 6.5 kills (*Mel Cozzens via Mark Styling*)

VF-6's second Hellcat tour in the frontline was badly affected by a serious *kamikaze* strike on *Hancock* off Okinawa on 7 April 1945, resulting in the squadron claiming just 20 victories (14 prior to the strike and six after returning in July), and producing no aces. This shot shows the surviving Hellcats being flown off to Maui on 21 April as the carrier limped towards Pearl Harbor for repairs (*Tailhook*)

the *Torch* landings, he used his F4F-4 to shoot down a Vichy French Curtiss Hawk 75A, plus a second fighter as a probable, over Morocco. During the squadron's *Essex* cruise in 1943-44 he added four Zeros and a 'Kate', then finished his last tour with a further three Japanese fighter kills in 1945. His nine victories over Axis aircraft included six different enemy types – Hawk 75A, 'Kate', 'Hamp'/Zeke, 'Nate', 'Jake' and 'Tony'.

**Okinawa Campaign** – *1 April to 23 June 1945*

**Top-Scoring F6F Squadrons**

| | | |
|---|---|---|
| VF-83 | *Essex* | 122 |
| VF-9 | *Yorktown* | 93.25 |
| VF-17 | *Hornet* | 89 |
| VF-30 | *Belleau Wood* | 77 |
| VBF-17 | *Hornet* | 76 |
| VBF-83 | *Essex* | 60 |
| VF-82 | *Bennington* | 60 |
| VF-47 | *Bataan* | 56.50 |
| VF-45 | *San Jacinto* | 45.50 |
| VBF-1 | *Randolph* | 45 |
| VBF-9 | *Yorktown* | 44 |

Total by 21 F6F squadrons – 837.25

**Top Hellcat Pilots of the Okinawa Campaign**

| | | | |
|---|---|---|---|
| Lt E A Valencia | VF-9 | 12.5 | Total 23 |
| Lt(jg) J B French | VF-9 | 10 | Total 11 |
| Lt(jg) H E Mitchell | VF-9 | 9 | Total 10 |
| Lt(jg) J M Johnston | VBF-17 | 8 | Total 9 |
| Ens C C Foster | VF-30 | 7.5 | Total 8.5 |

The Okinawan campaign also saw land-based Hellcats in the form of Marine F6F-5Ns taking a toll of Japanese nocturnal raiders, with two of the pilots in this group shot attaining ace status over the beleaguered island – Maj Bruce Porter, in the middle of the front row, and Capt Wally Sigler, to the former's left. Both pilots were flying with VMF(N)-542, and both had earlier scored the bulk of their kills in F4U-1s over the Solomons in 1943

Maj Porter's favoured mount, BuNo 78669, is readied for a sortie at Yontan in July 1945. Porter made ace in a rare double night kill on 15 June, using a mix of machine gun and cannon fire to down a *Ohka*-toting 'Betty' and a 'Nick' twin-engined fighter. Most nightfighting Hellcats kept the standard six-gun .5 cal armament – indeed, only Porter's -5N had cannon. Despite his success, most units experienced jamming problems with their cannon. Indeed, the Corps' only all-Hellcat night ace, Capt Robert Baird of VMF(N)-533, was able to use his 20 mms for just one of his six kills

Marine Corps nightfighter Hellcats also came into their own at Okinawa. Three Squadrons operating from Yontan and Kadena Airfields scored 69 kills, led by Lt Col Marion Magruder's VMF(N)-533, which accrued half of the total. The squadron also produced the Marine's only Hellcat ace, and also their only night ace – Capt Robert Baird, who shot down six aircraft during five interceptions in June and July.

Additionally, two former Corsair pilots became aces at Okinawa as VMF(N)-542's Maj Bruce Porter and Capt Wallace Sigler each logged their fifth victories while flying F6F-5Ns.

## Hellcat Nightfighter Squadrons at Okinawa – *April to August 1945*

| | |
|---|---|
| VMF(N)-533 | 35 |
| VMF(N)-542 | 18 |
| VMF(N)-543 | 16 |

'Old 76', as BuNo 78669 was known to its groundcrew, had been the chosen aircraft of Porter's predecessor, and as such nose-art in the form of a big red heart with the name 'Millie Lou' emblazoned across it. He immediately ordered that it be removed, and a 'big fifth of Schenley's whiskey', accompanied by the words *Black Death*, be applied in its place. Note the flash suppresser on the cannon muzzle

VMF(N)-533 'Crystal Gazers' was the most successful nightfighter unit in the Corps, downing 35 aircraft. Like most USMC Hellcats, BuNo 72627 wears nose-art on its cowling, and is in immaculate condition on Ie Shima on 27 June 1945. Marine Corps pilots initially felt that the Hellcat would make an inferior nightfighter when compared with the F4U-2 Corsair then being developed for the role, but the former soon proved to be the better machine in a combat environment (*Tailhook*)

# FLEET AIR ARM AND ANVIL-DRAGOON

I n British service the Hellcat had limited opportunity for aerial combat. However, since the Fleet Air Arm (FAA) only logged 455 aerial victories in six years of war, the F6F's contribution of 52 kills is not inconsiderable. In fact, American-built fighters accounted for more than one-third of the total, including 67 by Martlet/Wildcats and 52.5 by Corsairs.

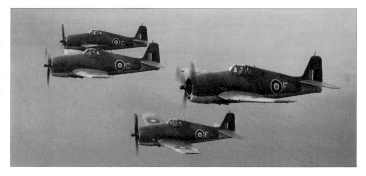

Originally, the Royal Navy called the F6F the 'Gannet', after a large seabird found in northern waters. The new Grumman was badly needed, as for a variety of political and economic reasons, Britain failed to field a satisfactory home-grown single-seat carrier fighter during the war. Granted, the Seafire Mk III was unquestionably the finest low-level naval fighter the Allies produced, but it lacked the range, offensive capability and, most importantly, carrier suitability of the rugged American types.

Beginning in the summer of 1943, the Royal Navy acquired the first of 1263 F6F-3s and -5s, called Gannet Mk Is and IIs, respectively. This little-used name was changed back to Hellcat in March 1944, by which time F6F-5N nightfighters were also becoming available.

Flying from the light carrier HMS *Emperor*, No 800 Sqn introduced the F6F to combat in British colours in December 1943. The occasion was a series of anti-shipping patrols along the Scandanavian coast, and Gannets were later charged with providing top cover for several large strikes against the German battleship *Tirpitz* during the following spring and summer.

Throughout these operations the only significant aerial combat experienced by FAA F6Fs occurred on 8 May 1944 when *Emperor's* Hellcats engaged a small number of Fw 190s and Bf 109Gs from JG 5 over Norway. Despite the *Luftwaffe* fighters' superior speed (30 kts or more), two Messerschmitts and a Focke-Wulf were claimed destroyed, the latter

A quarter of recently-arrived Gannet Is (later renamed Hellcats to avoid confusion with Britain's US allies) of No 800 Sqn patrol over the Irish Sea during a training sortie from Eglinton in September 1943. FAA Hellcats remained in this drab Dark Sea Grey/Extra Dark Sea Grey scheme throughout their time in Home Fleet service (*Charles E Brown*)

Lt Cdr Stanley Orr's No 804 Sqn found few problems in operating from the tiny deck of HMS *Emporer* in all but the fiercest of gales. Indeed, two squadrons of Hellcats (24 aircraft) were usually embarked during the Norwegian campaign in 1944 (*Stanley Orr*)

falling to veteran fighter pilot Lt Blyth Ritchie – the Scot joined the squadron in late 1941, and had been credited with 3.5 victories in Sea Hurricane Is and IICs in 1942.

On the 14th, Ritchie caught an ungainly Heinkel He 115 seaplane 'wave-hopping ' along the Norwegian coast and quickly shot it down, then joined seasoned ace, Lt Cdr Stanley G Orr, CO of No 804 Sqn, in splashing another – these kills made the Scot an ace, with his score standing at five destroyed and two shared destroyed, one damaged and one shared damaged. Sadly, Ritchie was killed in an operational accident soon after achieving this milestone.

## PILOT PROFILE

### Commander Stanley Orr DSC and two bars, AFC

Stanley Orr, like Blyth Ritchie, was also an ace, although he had achieved this status as early as November 1940, flying unwieldy Fairey Fulmar Is with No 806 Sqn in the Mediterranean aboard HMS *Illustrious*. When his carrier was badly damaged by German dive-bombers on 10 January 1941, Orr's squadron was put ashore at Malta, and he became one of the island's original defenders. Fighting pitched battles against overwhelming numbers of German and Italian fighters and bombers, the sub-lieutenant's score had risen to six destroyed and four shared by the time he returned to the UK in late 1941.

After a spell as an instructor, he was sent to America in August to take command on No 896 Sqn, which was forming on Martlets. Embarked aboard *Victorious*, the squadron sailed into the Pacific in March 1943, but Orr was struck down with polio and sent back to the UK. He made a full recovery, and in August of the same year was sent to RNAS Eglinton, in Northern Ireland, to take charge of No 804 Sqn, which was in the process of exchanging its veteran Sea Hurricane IICs for the FAA's first Hellcat Is (then called Gannets). Cdr Orr's experiences with the big Grumman, detailed in the following interview conducted specially for this volume by series editor Tony Holmes in October 1995, give the British side of the F6F story;

'The Hellcat was without a doubt the best, and most popular, naval fighter of the period. It suffered none of the Corsair's stall and visibility problems, being an easy aircraft both to fly and to deck land. It bestowed upon its pilot immense confidence, which was an important thing in those days as you usually had your hands more than full coping with the enemy! Indeed, it was such a stable platform to fly that following the *Tirpitz* raids we recommended that bomb racks be fitted to the aircraft. In no time at all this modification had been carried out, thus allowing us to attack targets on the

Lt Cdr Orr (left) and two of his pilots check their mission route prior to manning their Hellcats for the strike on *Tirpitz* on 3 April 1944. Note that all three naval aviators are wearing different flying gear, with perhaps the Bomber Command-style Irvin jacket adorning the pilot on the right being the most unusual. Most FAA aircrew preferred not to fly in their Irvins as they became water-logged should the wearer be forced to ditch. This photograph appeared on the front page of *The Evening News* (the forerunner of today's *Evening Standard*) on 8 April 1944 (*Stanley Orr*)

ground when we weren't required to act as fighter cover for our Barracudas and Avengers.

'In fact, following the departure of the larger fleet carriers following the big *Tungsten*, *Mascot* and *Goodwood* strikes in April, July and August 1944 respectively, the Norwegian campaign was left to the smaller escort carriers, whose principal strike aircraft was the Hellcat.

'Aside from its marvellous airborne attributes, the Hellcat also boasted an enviable reliability record. The aircraft rarely went unserviceable, which was crucially important as the escort carrier squadrons usually had only eight to ten Hellcats on strength at any one time – 50 per cent unserviceability could really hit your mission effectiveness!

'Unserviceability was one of the first problems I encountered with my new squadron at Eglinton when I arrived in August 1943, however. The unit's brand new Hellcat Is had only just arrived from America by ship, and had been sent ahead of the vessel carrying their spares! Despite this rather unfortunate state of affairs, we got on with our conversion to the fighter, but the first thing that happened was that the tailwheel tyres quickly began to wear out and burst due to our intensive programme of deck-landing practice.

'The squadron was on the verge of being permanently grounded when we came up with the idea of laminating strips of old truck tyre rubber together into a 12-in solid disc, which we then bolted onto our tailwheels – much to the chagrin of the FAA's engineering staff! Two months after our Hellcats had arrived, packing cases turned up with our long-awaited spares.

'We completed carrier qualification aboard *Ravager* in October 1943 and were then assigned to No 7 Naval Fighter Wing. A one-off convoy patrol to America aboard HMS *Emperor* then followed in December, and we used this trip both to thoroughly familiarise ourselves with the fighter around a carrier, and stock up with spares upon our arrival at Norfolk naval yard in Virginia in the New Year.

'Once we returned to the UK, we continued our training on the new fighter, both ashore and at sea, before heading north to Hatston, in the Orkneys, where we operated as a wing with other Barracuda and Avenger squadrons, rehearsing for the *Tungsten* strikes on *Tirpitz*. When the time came for the mission proper to be flown on 3 April 1944, we had practised the sortie so thoroughly that it all went like clockwork.

'The day dawned "gin clear", and No 804 Sqn was tasked with protecting the second strike on *Tirpitz*, which was to be performed by 19 Barracudas of No 52 Torpedo, Bomber, Reconnaissance (TBR) Wing an hour after the first attack – No 800 Sqn had helped escort the first assault. Six carriers were involved in the strike, with aircraft launching from a predetermined point 120 miles north-

**Hellcat I FN340 came to grief during No 804 Sqn's carrier qualification period aboard HMS *Ravager* when its pilot struck the stern of the ship on landing. Dated 22 October 1943, this accident was the only one suffered by the unit during its intensive 'blue water' shakedown cruise. The crestfallen pilot of FN340 can be seen to the right of the photo beneath the port wing roundel. This particular airframe was the first ever Hellcat flown by Lt Cdr Orr upon his arrival at No 804 Sqn, the new CO performing a brief familiarisation flight in the fighter on 12 August 1943 (*Stanley Orr*)**

west of Kaafjord. No less than 40 fighters, comprising Corsairs, Wildcats and Hellcats, provided the escort for the Wing, and my squadron took up station on the starboard side of the force.

'We experienced some difficulty in keeping station with the bombed-up Barracudas, which could barely make 135 kts. Some 20 miles from the coast, the strike force climbed to a height of 10,000 ft, and I positioned the Hellcats 1000 ft above them, weaving at about 190 kts. The squadron kept together well, with Green and White flights continually crossing over the centre section so as to keep an all-round lookout.

'Above us, the Corsairs seemed split up into groups of threes and fours which, in my opinion, would have made the immediate location of enemy fighters extremely difficult if there had been any around. Upon arrival over *Tirpitz*, it was found that the smoke screen generated by the Germans had risen half way up the mountains on either side of Kaafjord, but the heavy AA gun position Able was clear and firing repeatedly. Three or four other flak batteries were also shooting in our direction, so each flight attacked their pre-briefed gunsites once it was clear that no enemy fighters were in the area – I later heard a story after the war that most of the Luftwaffe fighter wing (JG 5) that was supposed to protect the battleship had returned briefly to Germany for re-equipment just days prior to the attack, and had been stuck there due to bad weather. However, I can't vouch for the truth of this tale!

'We dived from 8000 to 1000 ft at an angle of 50 degrees, firing three- to five-second bursts, and gun positions Able, Dog, Easy and Fox all temporarily fell silent. White section attempted to attack the smoke-obscured Baker AA site, and in so doing passed near to the stern of the *Tirpitz*, which was pouring smoke from its aft end. A flak and merchant ship were also strafed as the squadron flew out of the Kaafjord, before the flights reformed over the sea and proceeded to escort a number of Barracudas back to the task force at low-level.

'The Hellcat proved itself to be an excellent gunnery platform on this mission, and I wrote in my combat report to the captain of the *Emperor* on 5 April that "if we had been carrying bombs – the Hellcat is well suited for this purpose – we could possibly have contributed to the damage of the *Tirpitz*".

'Just over a month later we headed back into Norwegian waters in search of more targets of opportunity, and on 9 May we flew Operation *Hoop Dog* in search of a convoy near Gossen Island – I was leading eight Hellcats and a similar number of Wildcat Vs from *Searcher's* No 898 Sqn. We combed the area for a short time, but soon realised that there were no ships to be found, so I headed south. On passing over Fjortoft Island two Luftwaffe BV 138 floatplanes were spotted

Wearing its three-number serial crudely sprayed on its cowling, No 804 Sqn's JV145 is carefully positioned for launch from *Emperor* during the *Tirpitz* strikes. This type of hurried recognition marking was also seen on a number of F6F-3s in the Pacific in 1943/44, often being applied for ferry flights between land bases and the carrier task force (*Stanley Orr*)

taking off, so I ordered Black flight (comprising No 898 Sqn Wildcats) to attack, and both aircraft were quickly despatched – we were carrying bombs on our Hellcats, and thought it rather pointless to tackle the enemy in this configuration when we had the Wildcat Vs flying as fighter escorts.

'We then continued on with the sortie, and various targets ranging from oil tanks near Aalesund to a fish-oil factory and warehouse on an island off Kvalsvik were hit. A single Hellcat, flown by Kiwi Sub-Lt R A Cranwell, was lost to flak.

'On 14 May both Hellcats squadrons launched nine aircraft apiece as part of *Potluck Able* – a strike against enemy shipping off Rorvik. Eight of the Hellcats were configured as bombers and a similar number as fighters, whilst the remaining two aircraft carried out an armed recce of the target area five minutes prior to the strike force. As I led the formation in a climb to 5000 ft following landfall near Vikten Island, the recce pilots reported sighting several large ships off Rorvik.

'We ran into the target area from south to north, and whilst the Hellcat "fighters" strafed AA batteries in the harbour, I led the bomb-toting No 804 Sqn aircraft against two ships to the north of Rorvik, whilst the similarly-configured No 800 Sqn machines attacked two vessels to the south.

'Whilst all this was going on, No 800 Sqn's flight of four Hellcat "fighters" had sighted five He 115 floatplanes, whose pilots quickly realised they stood little chance against the marauding Grummans, and tried to alight on the water. Two Heinkels were shot down on the first pass – one fell to the guns of White flight leader, Lt Blyth Ritchie – and the remainder made panic landings north of Rorvik. Having successfully bombed our targets, I led Red Flight into the fight with the Heinkels, and I believe I made one pass at Ritchie's He 115 just prior to it crash-landing.

'By the time we had knocked our speed off and turned around to run in at them again, the three remaining floatplanes we bobbing up and down on the water like sitting ducks. White flight had since exhausted their ammunition after strafing the remaining He 115s, and it was left to us to finish them off – I shared in the sinking of one and then set another alight. A No 800 Sqn aircraft flown by Sub-Lt Hollway was hit by return fire from one of the He 115s and the pilot was forced to bale out on the return trip to *Emperor*. Sadly, he was never found.'

After D-Day No 804 Sqn was absorbed into No 800 Sqn, and duly disbanded – it later reformed on 1 September 1944 in South Africa on Hellcat IIs, prior to heading to the Far East where it saw more action. For Lt Cdr Orr, however, the 'shooting' war was over, being posted as Chief Flying Intructor to RNAS Henstridge in September 1944, before being accepted into the Empire Test Pilots' School at Boscombe Down – a move which was to feature prominantly in his postwar FAA career.

The He 115 successes on 14 May 1944 were the last aerial victories scored by the Hellcat against the Luftwaffe, despite Hellcat-equipped escort-carrier squadrons supporting the invasion of Southern France that August.

Royal Navy Hellcats were thrust into combat against Japan that same month when the East Indian Fleet launched strikes upon the Sumatran oilfields. Sporadic aerial combat occurred on 17-19 October, when Hellcats and Corsairs claimed seven 'Oscars' for three losses, including one F6F. Logging the first Pacific victories for British Hellcats were Sub-Lts E T Wilson and E Smithwick of *Indomitable's* No 1844 Sqn, the two pilots combining to destroy three 'Oscars'. The squadron added a 'Sally' bomber on 20 December.

Meanwhile, the FAA's only dedicated photo-reconnaissance unit in the region was also active at this time, No 888 Sqn flying Hellcat PR IIs (F6F-5Ps) from *Emperor*.

The heaviest aerial strikes flown against the Dutch East Indies occurred in December 1944 and January 1945, and included *Indomitable's* Nos 1839 and 1844 Sqns flying Hellcat Mk Is (F6F-3s) as part of No 5 Naval Fighter Wing. The *Meridian* strikes against petroleum targets around Palembang, though short in duration, evoked a serious response from the Japanese Army Air Force.

Three missions flown during late January brought a measure of success to FAA Hellcat pilots, with a trio of 'Oscars' being destroyed over Sumatra on 4 January, followed by five assorted fighters on the 24th and 5.5 victories on the 29th. All of these kills were recorded by *Indomitable's* two fighter squadrons, Nos 1839 and 1844 scoring four and 9.5 victories respectively. The most successful individual was Sub-Lt E T Wilson of the latter unit, with 2.5 kills.

*Indomitable's* monopoly on British Hellcat victories against Japan ended on 1 March. No 804 Sqn, still flying from the escort carrier *Emperor*, engaged Japanese Army aircraft off Rangoon, and seven pilots split two 'Oscars' and a 'Dinah' among them.

During the Okinawa and Home Island campaigns the British Pacific Fleet functioned as a semi-autonomous element of Task Force 38. There was a good deal of commonality, as both the US and British navies flew Hellcats, Corsairs and Avengers, while RN escort carriers also had Wildcats. However, the FAA also retained significant numbers of generic Barracuda, Firefly and Seafire aircraft.

On 8 April 1945 No 888 Sqn off HMS *Khedive* 'splashed' three snoopers which approached the task group, but AA guns and opera-

The top scoring Hellcat unit in the FAA by some considerable margin was No 1844 Sqn, whose pilots achieved 32.5 kills during their time aboard HMS *Indomitable* in 1944/45 – indeed, all six of the highest scoring Commonwealth Hellcat pilots saw service with this outfit. Initially equipped with Mk Is (F6F-3s), the unit was the recipient of some of the first Mk IIs (F6F-5s) delivered to the FAA in February 1945. These later aircraft were retained in their US Navy factory finish of overall Glossy Sea Blue, and the latter American-style roundels were also applied, as worn here on JZ935 (*Ray Sturtivant*)

tional crashes all took a toll in the last months of the war – both Nos 808 and 896 Sqns lost their COs in this way. The best day of the war for FAA Hellcats occurred on 12 April, whilst units were supporting strikes against Formosa. No 1844 Sqn splashed six enemy fighters, including two by Sub-Lt W M Foster.

Aerial combat largely eluded BPF Hellcats during May and June, with only three victories by *Indomitable* pilots on 4 May. On 25 July No 1844 Sqn made a high-altitude interception of four Aichi 'Grace' torpedo-bombers approaching the task group. Three were soon shot down, and the fourth escaped with a serious mauling. It was the Hellcat's final combat in British service. Of all the FAA fighter units involved in combat in the Far East, No 1844 sqn was clearly the highest scoring with 32.5 kills – next highest was the Corsair-equipped No 1836 Sqn with 17. The only other Hellcat unit to accrue a score of note was No 1839 Sqn with seven kills.

FAA pilots recorded only 18 aerial combats in Hellcats during the 15 months from May 1944 to July 1945, with the peak scoring period, not surprisingly, occurring during April of the latter year at the time of the Okinawa invasion. No less than 19 of the Hellcat's 52 victories were logged in that month alone.

At the end of the war the FAA boasted 12 Hellcat squadrons split between Home Stations, the East Indian and Pacific Fleets. Though not the most successful Royal Navy fighter, the Hellcat surely proved itself one of the most versatile.

### Top FAA Hellcat Units

| No 1844 Sqn | *Indomitable* | 32.5 |
|---|---|---|
| No 1839 Sqn | *Indomitable* | 7 |
| No 800 Sqn | *Emperor* | 5.5 |
| No 808 Sqn | *Khedive* | 4 |
| No 804 Sqn | *Emperor* | 3 |

### Top FAA Hellcat Pilots

| Sub-Lt E T Wilson | No 1844 Sqn | 4.83 |
|---|---|---|
| Sub-Lt W M Foster | No 1844 Sqn | 4.50 |
| Lt W H Atkinson | No 1844 Sqn | 3.33 |
| Sub-Lt R F Mackie | No 1839/1844 | 3 |
| Sub-Lt W Fenwick-Smith | No 1844 Sqn | 3 |
| Sub-Lt MacLennan | No 1844 Sqn | 3 |

## ANVIL-DRAGOON

The Hellcat's only European combat in US service occurred in an unlikely venue  the stylish vacation coast of Southern France. Two months after the Normandy landings the Anglo-American operation called *Anvil-Dragoon* (the code-name was changed just before the commencement of 'D-Day South') initiated a giant pincer against German forces in Occupied Europe. Assault troops went ashore on 15 August.

Whilst huge carrier battles were raging in the Pacific that often involved hundreds of Hellcats, a modest force of two 10,400-ton *Casablanca* class escort carriers combined with two small Royal Navy 'flattops' to support the Allied invasion of Southern France in mid-August 1944. Two US Navy Hellcat units were involved – VOF-1 aboard USS *Tulagi*, who were tasked primarily with target spotting for naval gunners, and VF-74 embarked on USS *Kasaan Bay*. This photograph shows a bomb-toting F6F-5 of the latter unit being launched on a close-air support sortie on 15 August. Four days later elements of VF-74 downed a Ju 88 and a Do 217 attempting to bomb Task Force 88. The unit flew 289 sorties in 11 days in support of Operation *Dragoon*, losing five aircraft in the process (*Tailhook*)

Supporting the landings were two American escort carriers, each operating an independent F6F-5 squadron. Embarked in *Kasaan Bay* was Lt Cdr H B Bass's VF-74 while Lt Cdr W F Bringle took VOF-1 (Observation-Fighter) aboard *Tulagi*. The latter unit was specially trained in artillery and naval gunfire spotting, which was a skill much in demand for an amphibious operation.

In concert with British carrier squadrons, the Hellcats' primary missions were close air support, interdiction and gunnery spotting. However, a handful of aerial encounters developed, and the F6F pilots made the most of their limited opportunities.

Two combats occurred on 19 August – the second anniversary of the Dieppe landing in northern France – with Lt Cdr Bass and his division downing a Junkers Ju 88 in the morning, followed in the afternoon by two *Kasaan Bay* pilots shooting down a Dornier Do 217 north-east of Issiore. No other *Luftwaffe* aircraft presented themselves to 'Fighting 74', but Bass was shot down and killed by flak – one of 11 US Hellcats lost in the operation.

Bringle's *Tulagi* pilots claimed six victories – three Heinkel He 111s fell near Vienne on the evening of the 19th, followed by three Junkers Ju 52 transports on the 21st. Top scorer was Ens Edward W Olszewski who downed two of the latter despite having only one operable gun. He and three others added to their Axis tallies against Japan in 1945 flying FM-2 Wildcats with the redesignated VOC-1.

## Top Hellcat scores of *Anvil-Dragoon*

| | | |
|---|---|---|
| Ens Edward W Olszewski | VOF-1 | 2 |
| Ens Alfred R Wood | VOF-1 | 1.5 |
| Ens Richard V Yentzer | VOF-1 | 1 |

Eight other VOF-1 and VF-74 pilots scored partial victories.

# END GAME

The final phase of the Pacific War began in early July 1945. With the Imperial Navy long removed as a threat, carrier task groups were free to concentrate on strike operations against coastal and shore-based targets, including Japanese industry. Hoarding remaining aircraft and aircrews for the expected invasion, Japan ceded air superiority to the Allies. Consequently, aerial combat dropped dramatically, with naval aviators claiming 265 shootdowns in May, compared with a mere 20 in June. However, the final series of strikes, especially against remaining enemy fleet units, prompted a brief resurgence in July.

Aerial combat only occurred on six days of that month, with 56 of the total 59 kills being claimed on the 24th, 25th and 28th. The latter three dates involved strikes against naval targets at Kure, Kobe and elsewhere in the Inland Sea. Japan's remaining battleships and aircraft carriers, lacking fuel and air cover, lay immobile and open to attack almost at will.

These operations marked the return of some veteran squadrons. 'Fighting Six' was back in the repaired *Hancock* while VF-16 arrived for a second deployment, now aboard *Randolph*. Both units scored on the 24th, but VF-31, also newly returned to combat, starred the next day. The *Belleau Wood* pilots claimed eight kills over Yokaichi Airfield, four 'Franks' falling to Lt(jg) C N Nooy – despite this action being his only aerial combat of his second cruise, it raised his wartime total to 19 confirmed.

Also back was VF-27, displaced from *Princeton* in October. Now aboard *Independence*, Lt Cdr Bardshar's unit was back in combat in May – a turnaround period of only seven months. He found Home Island operations both bigger and better organised than was previously the case.

'During July and August 1945 we hit Kure, Niigata, Muroran, Yokosuka and Utsunomiya, among others. Kure's defenses were, I think, the strongest and certainly the most spectacular. They used coloured bursts for air spotting as we did with surface naval rifles. Concern with flak at Kure was somewhat tempered by concern with mid-air collisions. The raids were large, rather well co-ordinated and concentrated, and the density of US aircraft over the targets was high.'

On 28 July Hellcat pilots accounted for another 22 airborne bandits, including 13 by VF-16. That morning a dozen 'Franks' were claimed, including three by Lt Cleveland R Null and one by Lt John W Bartol. They became the last ever Hellcat aces, raising their respective scores to seven and five – their previous kills dated from 1943.

Following the atomic bombs drops on Hiroshima and Nagasaki on 6 and 9 August, TF-38 sailors and fliers anxiously awaited Japan's response. When no surrender was forthcoming, the carrier men urged their Army Air Force counterparts

Wearing distinctive rudder stripes and boasting all-white ailerons, the F6F-5s of VF-/VBF-12 were amongst the most colourful Hellcats in the Pacific in 1945. Based aboard USS *Randolph*, the 'twinned' squadrons boasted a combined fleet of nearly 60 fighters, and between them downed 125 aircraft in five months of near-solid action in Japanese home waters – pilots from the VBF unit actually outscored their VF rivals 74 to 51. Twelve aces flew with the squadrons on this tour, with six achieving this much coveted status during the 1945 deployment (*US Navy*)

Air Group 16 relieved Air Group 12 aboard *Randolph* at Leyte Gulf on 17 June 1945, and returned to the frontline the following month. By this stage in the war, aerial opposition had all but disappeared, so it came as something of a surprise when an eight-strong flight of VF-16 F6Fs was tackled by a large force of 'Franks' and 'Georges' over Ozuki on 28 July. Twelve 'Franks' and a solitary 'George' were downed without a single Hellcat being lost. Two pilots made aces during this action – Lt C L Null, whose trio of 'Franks' added to his four kills from VF-16's 1943/44 det; and Lt J W Bartol, who bagged a 'Frank' to take his tally to five. The plane-guard destroyer in this shot is HMS *Verulam* (*US Navy*)

Veterans of some of the first action seen by the Hellcat in the Pacific at Tarawa in late 1943, VF-1 returned to the frontline aboard USS *Bennington* in time to witness the death throes of Japan. Indeed, so spent a force was their once formidable enemy that only a solitary kill (a 'Judy' on 13 August) was scored on this tour. Photographed in early August, Hellcat BuNo 71351 still displays *Bennington*'s distinctive 'Christmas Tree' 'G'-symbol on its tail and ailerons, despite the carrier having been issued with the more mundane 'TT' codes the previous month (*US Navy*)

to drop one or two more A-bombs, hoping to hasten the war's end. Instead, the endless routine of strikes and CAPs continued as before.

In the 30 days preceding the surrender – 14 July to 14 August – 89 Japanese aircraft fell to Navy pilots, this tally representing 24 units, of which 14 claimed 65 kills. With more opportunity than the others, VF-16 and -31 easily led the month-long scoring tally with 18 and 12 victories, respectively.

On the morning of 15 August, strikes were inbound to Japan when an urgent recall order was radioed. Emperor Hirohito had decreed surrender, leading to an order for the immediate cessation of hostilities. It was very much a mixed blessing. While most airborne pilots and crews gleefully dropped their ordnance offshore and returned to their carriers, others were fighting for their lives. VF-31 tangled with Zekes offshore and splashed six while *San Jacinto's* VF-49 claimed seven more A6M5s west of Mito. About the same time VF-6 shot three fighters into Sagami Bay, just before the imperial announcement.

However, VF-88 was jumped near Atsugi and was forced to fight some determined, aggressive, 'Franks' and 'Jacks'. Nine Japanese fell to the outnumbered *Yorktown* pilots, who lost four of their number.

The task force reinforced the CAP, now alerted to other recalcitrant Japanese aviators. Between 1120 and 1400, Corsairs shot down two intruders while VF-86 Hellcats off *Wasp* splashed another pair. The last Hellcat victory of the day was also the last of World War 2, Ens Clarence A Moore beating the remaining elements of his VF-31 division to gun range and duly despatching a 'Judy' dive-bomber at 1400. It was Moore's first victory, and the Hellcat's 5271st by Allied pilots.

**Top F6F Squadrons** – July to August 1945

|        |                   |    |
|--------|-------------------|----|
| VF-31  | *Belleau Wood*    | 19 |
| VF-16  | *Randolph*        | 18 |
| VF-88  | *Yorktown*        | 13 |
| VF-49  | *San Jacinto*     | 12 |
| VFN-91 | *Bon Homme Richard* | 9 |
|        |                   |    |
|        | Total by 13 squadrons – | 88 |

**Top-Scoring Hellcat Pilots** – July to August 1945

|               |          |   |          |
|---------------|----------|---|----------|
| Lt J A Gibson | VF-49    | 4 | Total 4  |
| Ens P T McDonald | VF(N)-91 | 4 | Total 4 |
| Lt C N Nooy   | VF-31    | 4 | Total 19 |
| Lt C L Null   | VF-16    | 3 | Total 7  |
| Lt(jg) M Proctor | VF-88 | 3 | Total 3  |
| Lt(jg) G M Williams | VF-49 | 3 | Total 3 |

# WARTIME HISTORY OF VF-19

Fighting Squadron 19 was established at Naval Auxiliary Air Station Los Alamitos, California, on 15 August 1943. The commanding officer, Lt Cdr T Hugh Winters, was born and bred a Navy man; his father, T H Winters, Sr, had graduated from Annapolis in 1909, and was 25 years old when baby Hugh was born in South Carolina on 11 March 1913.

Winters graduated in the Naval Academy class of 1935, a prime year group for combat in World War 2. Two won the Medal of Honour, including one posthumously – in total, some 40 of Winters' classmates perished during the War, including 15 as aviators. Members of the 'Class of '35' died at Pearl Harbor, Coral Sea and Midway, whilst fellow fighter aces included Fred Bakutis (VF-20), Leonard 'Duke' Davis (VMF-121), Noel Gayler (VF-3), Eddie Outlaw (VF-32), Gordon Schechter (VF-45) and Malcolm Wordell (VF-44).

When VF-19 'stood up', Winters 'owned' one F6F-3, a J2F-5 Duck amphibian and a Piper Cub. By early September there were seven Hellcats, with 29 on hand by year's end.

In seeking a name, the squadron decided upon a way of honouring its aircraft. Therefore, 'Fighting 19' became 'Satan's Kittens,' and the name remained for three-and-a-half decades. The emblem was designed by Walt Disney Studios, and showed an angry, caped, cat astride an airborne spear holding lightning bolts in one paw.

Winters' pilots were not representative of most newly-established fighting squadrons, as his aviators included several senior- and junior-grade lieutenants happy to be out of instructing billets, some cast-offs from other squadrons, and a few former dive-bomber and floatplane pilots.

Because new *Essex*-class carriers experienced some inevitable 'slippage' in reaching the fleet, Air Group 19 had time on its hands. In seeking diversions, VF-19's intelligence officer, Lt Jack Wheeler, acquired a slot machine. Instead of mundane cherries, bells and fruit

VF-19's commissioning CO, and later its CAG, Cdr Hugh Winters, Jr, was an inspirational leader of men who was in the thick of combat throughout Air Group 19's *Lexington* deployment in 1944. He claimed eight kills and one probable during his time in the frontline, using two identically marked F6F-5s christened *HANGER LILLY* – Winters also had a flightdeck tractor similarly adorned with both this sobriquet and his familiar 'Mohawk 99' modex. This photograph was taken in late October 1944, just days prior to CAG-19 scoring his eighth, and last, kill – an 'Oscar' downed on an anti-shipping strike over Manila Bay on 5 November
(*Hugh Winters via Mark Styling*)

gum, this device was altered to ring up Zekes, 'Bettys' and 'Vals'. Officially the 'one-armed bandit' was dubbed the 'Visual Aid Recognition Machine', or 'VARM' for short.

Prior to the creation of VF-19, Los Alamitos had been a pleasantly dull little field where nothing much happened. As an elimination-training base, it allowed aviation cadets to 'bounce' in Stearman N2S biplanes, while all hands adopted genteel manners in keeping with Navy Regulations.

However, it did not take long for the unconventional Hugh Winters, or his boys, to stand out from the crowd. One pilot was caught running from a hangar to bachelor officers' quarters, wearing flight gear. This was bad enough, but the culprit failed to halt when challenged by the duty petty officer. Then, when the base commander tried to confiscate 'VARM', Winters decided enough was enough. He flew down to NAS San Diego and straightened things out with Commander, Fleet Air. After explaining the importance of 'VARM' to VF-19's morale and efficiency (not to mention the squadron party fund), a compromise was reached. 'Fighting 19' could keep the controversial gadget if Winters would accept two lieutenants (junior grade) whom no other squadron wanted.

One of the miscreants was unable to get aboard a carrier at night and the other had made an unauthorized landing at Anaheim. Winters quickly agreed, saying, 'I've got worse than that putting 60 holes in the banner target'. VF-19 continued its 'recognition training' and then carrier-qualified aboard *Altamaha* (CVE-18).

By the end of February 1944, Air Group 19 was headed for Hawaii as passengers aboard *Lexington*. Winters and company established itself on Maui and concentrated on gunnery, formation and instrument flying, as well as the obligatory socialising. The unit was dealt a cruel blow in late March when 20 pilots were ordered to VF-100 – the fleet fighter pool – and were replaced by less well-trained aviators. Many of the new men had never flown an F6F, but they were quickly assimilated into the squadron as wingmen and generally proved capable.

The squadron was shaping up well. Air discipline and radio procedures were good, and gunnery scores stood above average. Satan's Kittens were combat ready, but officialdom proved difficult. During a blackout two VF-19 ensigns 'borrowed' the base executive officer's jeep and proceeded to the Maui *Shimbun*, 'a happy place where the girls served saki and stuff'. Quickly retrieved by the shore patrol, the errant aviators faced possible return to the US, but 'skipper' Winters took punitive action by immediately grounding the pilots – from operating jeeps! His judgment proved correct, as both offenders finished the tour as aces.

The air group rode *Intrepid* to Eniwetok at the end of June and, on 9 July, flew aboard *Lexington* in Task Group 38.3. 'Lady Lex' would be VF-19's home for the next four months, the most important 120 days in the squadron's 35-year history. 'Satan's Kittens' embarked upon their combat cruise with a full complement of 37 F6F-3s, including two -3P 'photo birds'.

With only four combat-experienced pilots, including Winters, the squadron flew its first missions during strikes on Guam between 18 and 21 July. The Hellcats were armed with 500-lb bombs on nearly every flight, and encountered no enemy aircraft. Although Japanese AA fire was described as 'light,' it could not be discounted, as VF-19 lost two pilots during this period.

During late July and early August, strikes were launched against the Palaus and Bonins. A VF-19 photo pilot, Lt John Hutto, tangled with a Rufe over Urukthapol on 25 July and claimed it probably destroyed. In the latter missions on 4 and 5 August, VF-19 scored its first confirmed victories – two Zekes shot down near Iwo Jima, scored almost one year after forming at Los Alamitos. But, according to the squadron history, the flak was 'by far the most severe yet experienced'. Three pilots and four F6Fs were lost, including Lt H R Burnett, previously one of the fleet's finest SBD pilots. He had shot down two Japanese aircraft in the Solomons during 1942.

Despite the losses, morale remained high as the pilots participated in flightdeck athletics and anticipated large-scale combat. Their training stressed deflection shooting, and most felt confident that they would do well against Japanese aircraft. But squadron doctrine emphasised the importance of teamwork. As Winters said, 'On CAP: keep quiet, listen and look. On escort: no VF pilot can ever leave his VB or VT to shoot down planes that are not committing to attack same, or you'.

With the invasion of the Philippines, these concepts were put to good use. The first day of the operation was 9 September, when Winters led his Hellcats from *Lexington* to shoot up Japanese airfields in the Cagayan Vally of Mindanao. Twenty-seven enemy aircraft were claimed destroyed on the ground.

Three days later VF-19 got in its first large dogfight and won 14 to nothing. Topguns were Lt Albert Seckel with four kills and Winters with three.

As the fast carriers sent strikes over the length of the Philippines, VF-19 ranged far afield. Over 30 aircraft were strafed on Cebu during 12 September, a pattern that was set to continue during the next 48 hours as a further 80 were claimed destroyed on airfields on Negros and Panay Islands. Some of these missions involved round trips of 600 nautical miles. Following the injury of CAG Cdr Karl Jung during a ditching near the task force, Cdr Winters 'fleeted up' to become CAG-19. On 10 October, he intercepted a twin-engine Japanese aircraft 30 miles west of the task force. He closed the range, identified it as a 'Fran', and easily shot it down. Thus began the most successful 30 days in the history of American fighter aviation, that 'Fran' being the first of 1229 enemy aircraft credited to US Navy squadrons during the month.

Personally-assigned aircraft were unusual on the *Essex*-class carriers, owing to the near impossibility of properly 'spotting' (positioning) a pilot's assigned machine on the deck

'Satan's Kittens' relax in their ready room awaiting the call the main their aircraft in October 1944. The pilots visible in the front rows are, from left to right; Lt(jg) Clarence E Bartlett (one kill); a cigar-chewing Lt Roger S Boles (four kills); Lt(jg) Israel H Silvert (two kills); Lt(jg) 'Moose' Dawson; Lt 'Lin' Lindsay (eight kills); and Ens William H Martin (four kills) (*Elvin Lindsay*)

Lt(jg) Ed Copeland was one of 11 aces produced by VF-19 during their solitary frontline tour, having joined the unit soon after it was established at Los Alamitos in mid-1943. Five of Copeland's eventual tally of six kills were scored in two actions – he downed an 'Oscar' and a 'Nate' over central Formosa on the morning of 12 October 1944, and bagged a 'Nell', a 'Betty' and a 'Lily' 12 days later over Luzon, again on a morning sweep. Any chance of adding to this tally was dashed on 6 November when Copeland was shot down by AA gunners over Manila. Fortunately, he was rescued by Filipino guerrillas and returned to VF-19 on New Year's Eve (*Ed Copeland via Mark Styling*)

for launch. However, the exception to this rule was provided by air group commanders, and as CAG-19, Winters had a pet Hellcat. The combination of *Lexington's* call sign and the CAG side number rendered his airborne identity as '99 Mohawk'.

However, number 99 gained another identity, as the plane captain dubbed the F6F-5 *Hanger Lilly*, with an appropriate flower emblem. Despite the spelling error (referring to the hangar deck), '*Lilly* became a notable fixture, spotted at the head of almost every major mission flown by Air Group 19. When Winters' first CAG bird was jettisoned with battle damage, his plane captain, John Uhoch, quickly produced a duplicate, complete with both name and artwork.

Winters was succeeded as CO of VF-19 by Lt Cdr Franklin E Cook, Jr, who led 'Satan's Kittens' against Formosa on 12 October. It was the squadron's hardest combat to date. Outnumbered as much as six to one, the *Lexington* Hellcats claimed 28.5 kills for the loss of two pilots and three aircraft, with several other F6Fs damaged. One of the missing fliers was Lt Cdr Cook, who was replaced by the next senior pilot, Lt Roger Boles. Three small combats later in the day raised the squadron tally to 33.5 victories. The 'Kittens'' first aces were crowned on 12 October as Cdr Winters and Lt Joseph J Paskoski logged their fifth aerial victories. Lt(jg) William J Masoner, Jr, dropped three Zekes on this day which, combined with two prior victories scored with VF-11 in 1943, also made him an ace. Two days later Lt(jg) Luther D Prater ran his score to 5.5 victories, all with VF-19.

Undoubtedly, the two busiest days in the squadron's history were 24-25 October 1944, otherwise known as the Battle of Leyte Gulf. On the 24th the squadron had expanded to 41 Hellcats, including 24 new F6F-5s. In addition to its two-aircraft photo section, VF-19 also now boasted a flight of three nightfighter Hellcats as well. To find employment for all these aircraft, 'Fighting 19' sent search teams across the central Philippines looking for Japanese fleet units and targets of opportunity. On one of these searches north of Manila, Lt Masoner hit the aerial jackpot. He came across four hostile formations and shot down six twin-engined aircraft (four 'Nells', a 'Dinah' and a 'Betty'), all confirmed by gun camera. The rest of his division accounted for a further seven aircraft, including three which fell to his wingman, Ens William E Copeland. Besides Masoner and Copeland, three other VF-19 aces emerged from the day's combats. They included Lt Elvin L Lindsay, whose team met heavy fighter opposition over Clark Field and shot down ten bandits. In all, VF-19 search teams had claimed 30 victories.

Meanwhile, TG-38.3 was coming under heavy attack. A scramble was ordered, and as VF-19 pilots sprinted down the flightdeck to man aircraft, 'Lex's' AA gunners actually cheered them on. Lt Boles' Hellcats splashed a dozen raiders during this attack, although the F6F CAP failed to prevent the light carrier *Princeton* from being mortally damaged.

By mid-morning CAG Winters was leading a strike against Japanese warships in the Sibuyan Sea. The fighters strafed to suppress flak as the carrier bombers attacked under low clouds which restricted visibility. During this mission, and subsequent flights, another 12 bandits were splashed, which helped establish a squadron record of 52 kills and nine probables during a single day's operations, against the loss of one pilot.

Twenty-four hours later Cdr Winters was again target co-ordinator, directing several strikes against the Japanese carrier force off Cape Engano, Luzon. The targets were one heavy and three light carriers, plus two battleships and several escorts. Air opposition was weak, but Lt Boles downed a Zero while leading an attack against a CVL. *Lexington* aircraft were credited with shares in sinking or damaging four enemy warships, as VF-19 had attacked with bombs.

A brief study of just one pilot's activity during this period indicates the sustained nature of VF-19's operations. From 22 September to 25 October Lt Bruce W Williams shot down seven enemy aircraft, bombed a battleship and won the Navy Cross, three DFCs and the Air Medal. A pre-war law student from Salem, Oregon, Williams got to fighters via OS2Us. Because *Lexington's* callsign was 'Mohawk', Williams became known in the task force as 'Willy Mohawk'.

During this time, Williams was flying a damaged Hellcat back from a bombing mission 'clear to hell and gone west of Palawan'. Concerned that the task group would have departed the prebriefed recovery site, he tried a maximum-range radio call, 'This is "Willie Mohawk". I'm hit and I'm trying to make it in.' When he reached Point Option, 'Lady Lex' was still there to take him aboard. Bruce Williams felt that Vice Adm Marc Mitscher, riding in *Lexington*, had kept the force steaming west in order to retrieve the lone Hellcat pilot.

On 5 November Lt Boles led a fighter sweep over Luzon, and Lt Herman J Rossi made ace. However, 'Smiley' Boles was hit by AA fire and crashed south of Manila. He was succeeded by 25-year-old Lt Elvin Lindsay. 'Lin' Lindsay became VF-19's third skipper in three weeks – undoubtedly the youngest squadron CO in the US Navy.

Whilst the Luzon raid was occuring four suicide Zekes attacked *Lexington*. AA gunners splashed three, but the fourth proved both determined and skilful. He struck astern of the island, to starboard, killing 50 men, including 11 from the air group.

The next day the 'Kittens' flamed 13 bandits, raising Lt Albert Seckel and Ens R A Farnsworth to acedom. Seckel got an 'Oscar', then chased an unidentified single-engined fighter to sugar-cane level where the enemy pilot bailed out. With his parachute streaming, the luckless Japanese smashed into a tree. Later it was determined that VF-19 had shot down the first Kawanishi N1K 'George' to fall to allied fire. Farnsworth made ace the hard way, taking the wing off a 'Tojo' in a mid-air collision, but another pilot was lost during the sweep – the 16th attributed to enemy action.

*Lexington* returned to Ulithi, expecting to head out soon, but

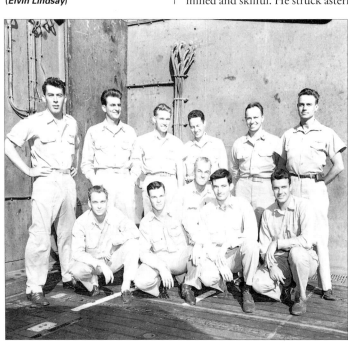

Ed Copeland was still evading capture in the jungles of Luzon when this shot of the remaining ten aces in VF-19 was taken in December 1944. Standing, left to right, are; Lt B W Williams (seven kills), Lt J J Paskoski (six kills), Lt E L Lindsay (eight kills), Cdr T H Winters (eight kills), Lt W J Masoner (12 kills) and H J Rossi, Jr, (six kills). Kneeling, left to right, are; Lt A Seckel (six kills), Ens P O'Mara (seven kills), Lt J Wheeler (Air Combat Intelligence Officer), Ens R A Farnsworth (five kills) and Lt(jg) L D Prater (8.5 kills) (*Elvin Lindsay*)

word arrived informing Cdr Winters that Air Group 19's tour was over. The 'Kittens', with their bomber and 'torpecker' shipmates, would be home for Christmas.

By the end of the deployment, 38 VF-19 pilots were credited with 155 confirmed victories and 16 probables. The 11 aces claimed 76.5 kills, or very nearly half the squadron total. Almost 200 more enemy aircraft were thought to have been destroyed on the ground. 'Satan's Kittens' were awarded 98 combat decorations, comprising 16 Navy Crosses, nine Silver Stars, 32 DFCs, 25 Air Medals and 16 Purple Hearts.

But more importantly, Winters' goal of perfection in the escort role was met – not one Air Group 19 Helldiver or Avenger was lost to Japanese fighters. In fact 'Torpedo 19' claimed two shootdowns and 'Bombing 19' an exceptional 11 – probably the highest among all SB2C units.

'Fighting 19' began the New Year by reforming at NAS Alameda, near San Francisco, in February 1945. The new commanding officer was Lt Cdr Joseph G Smith. In keeping with the revised carrier air group composition, a fighter-bomber squadron was formed from VF-19, designated VBF-19 with F4U Corsairs.

Upon moving to NAAS Santa Rosa in May, 'Satan's Kittens' became the first squadron to receive F8F-1 Bearcats. After completion of further training, VF-19 boarded the light carrier *Langley*, once more Hawaii-bound. Arriving on 8 August, the squadron set up additional training but the war was rapidly winding down. On the 15th – the squadron's second anniversary – the Japanese agreed to unconditional surrender, and VF-19's war was over.

What the well-equipped fighter ace used for transport when out of the cockpit. Lt 'Lin' Lindsay became the CO of VF-19 at just 25, following the death in combat over Manila of 'Smiley' Boles on 5 November 1944. This shot was taken early in 1945 whilst Lindsay was helping to establish the newly-formed VBF-19 in Hawaii. The aircraft is an F4U-4, as operated by his new unit, whilst the motorcycle is an Indian (*Elvin Lindsay*)

| VF-19 Aces | |
| --- | --- |
| Lt W J Masoner, Jr | 10 (+2 in F4Fs with VF-11) |
| Lt(jg) L D Prater | 8.5 |
| Lt E.L. Lindsay | 8 |
| Cdr T H Winters | 8 |
| Ens P O'Mara, Jr | 7 |
| Lt B W Williams | 7 |
| Ens W E Copeland | 6 |
| Lt J J Paskoski | 6 |
| Lt H J Rossi, Jr | 6 |
| Lt A Seckel, Jr | 6 |
| Ens R A Farnsworth, Jr | 5 |

# APPENDICES

## Top-Scoring Pacific Escort Carrier F6F Units

| | | | |
|---|---|---|---|
| VF-60 | *Suwannee* | 1943-44 | 25 |
| VF-37 | *Sangamon* | 1943-44 | 20 |
| VF-35 | *Chenango* | 1943-44 | 9 |
| VF-40 | *Suwannee* | 1945 | 9 (+20 previously*) |
| VF-24 | *Santee* | 1945 | 3 (+34.5 previously*) |
| VF-25 | *Chenango* | 1945 | 3 (+34 previously*) |

*Previous scores achieved whilst land-based or aboard light carriers

## Top-Scoring Pacific CVE Hellcat Pilots

| | | |
|---|---|---|
| Lt(jg) K W Kenyon | VF-37 | 4 |
| Lt(jg) R A Singleton | VF-60 | 3.25 |
| Ens J E Donnelly | VF-37 | 3 |
| Lt Cdr J C Longino | VF-40 | 3 |

## Top 25 Hellcat Units 1943-1945

| | | |
|---|---|---|
| VF-15 | *Essex* | 310 |
| VF-9 | *Essex, Lexington, Yorktown* | 250.75 |
| VF-2 | *Enterprise, Hornet* | 248 |
| VF-18 | *Intrepid* | 176.5 |
| VF-31 | *Cabot, Belleau Wood* | 165.60 |
| VF-17 | *Hornet* | 161 |
| VF-30 | *Belleau Wood, Monterey* | 159.83 |
| VF-80 | *Ticonderoga, Hancock* | 159.50 |
| VF-20 | *Enterprise, Lexington* | 158.16 |
| VF-8 | *Bunker Hill* | 156 |
| VF-19 | *Lexington* | 155 |
| VF-16 | *Lexington, Randolph* | 154.50 |
| VF-14 | *Wasp* | 147 |
| VF-83 | *Essex* | 137 |
| VF-27 | *Princeton, Independence* | 135 |
| VF-5 | *Yorktown* | 126.50 |
| VBF-17 | *Hornet* | 121 |
| VF-29 | *Cabot* | 113 |
| VBF-12 | *Randolph* | 109 |
| VF-11 | *Hornet* | 103 |
| VF-1 | *Yorktown* | 101 |
| VF-33 | Solomons and *Sangamon* | 90.50 |
| VF-10 | *Enterprise* | 88 |
| VF-13 | *Franklin* | 86 |
| VF-82 | *Bennington* | 85 |
| **Total** | | **3696.84** |

## Top Hellcat Aces

| | | | |
|---|---|---|---|
| Cdr David McCampbell | VF-15 | 34 | Twice ace in a day |
| Lt Eugene A Valencia | VF-9 | 23 | 6 on 17/4/45 |
| Lt Cecil E Harris | VF-18 | 22 | Plus 1 in F4Fs |
| Lt Patrick D Fleming | VF-80 | 19 | 5 on 16/2/45 |
| Lt Cornelius Nooy | VF-31 | 19 | 5 on 21/9/44 |
| Lt Alexander Vraciu | VF-6/-16 | 19 | 6 on 19/6/44 |
| Lt(jg) Douglas Baker | VF-20 | 16.333 | KIA 14/12/44 |
| Lt Arther R Hawkins | VF-31 | 14 | 5 on 13/9/44 |
| Lt John L Wirth | VF-31 | 14 | |
| Lt Cdr George C Duncan | VF-15 | 13.5 | |
| Lt(jg) Roy W Rushing | VF-15 | 13 | 6 on 24/10/44 |
| Lt John R Strane | VF-15 | 13 | |
| Lt(jg) Wendell V Twelves | VF-15 | 13 | |
| Lt Daniel A Carmichael | VF-2/VBF-12 | 12 | |
| Lt Cdr Hamilton McWhorter III | VF-9/-12 | 12 | First F6F ace |
| Lt James A Shirley | VF-27 | 12 | 5 on 24/10/44 |
| Lt Clement M Craig | VF-22 | 11.75 | 5 on 21/1/45 |
| Lt(jg) George R Carr | VF-15 | 11.5 | 5 on 19/6/44 |
| William A Dean, Jr | VF-2 | 11 | |
| Lt(jg) James B French | VF-9 | 11 | |
| Lt Harvey P Picken | VF-18 | 11 | 5 on 21/9/44 |
| Ens James V Reber, Jr | VF-30 | 11 | |
| Lt Cdr James Rigg | VF-15 | 11 | 5 on 12/9/44 |
| Lt Cdr Marshall U Beebe | VF-17 | 10.5 | 5 on 18/3/45 |
| Lt Carl A Brown, Jr | VF-27 | 10.5 | 5 on 24/10/44 |
| Lt(jg) Robert E Murray | VF-29 | 10.333 | |
| Lt Cdr Leonard J Check | VF-7 | 10 | |
| Lt Thaddeus T Coleman, Jr | VF-6/-83 | 10 | |
| Lt(jg) Charles M Mallory | VF-18 | 10 | 5 on 21/9/44 |
| Lt William J Masoner, Jr | VF-19 | 10 | Plus 2 in F4Fs |
| Lt(jg) Harris E Mitchell | VF-9 | 10 | |
| Lt(jg) Arthur Singer, Jr | VF-15 | 10 | |
| Lt Armistead B Smith, Jr | VF-9/VBF-12 | 10 | |
| Lt James Stewart | VF-31 | 10 | |
| Lt Charles R Stimpson | VF-11 | 10 | 5 on 14/10/44 |
| | | | Plus 6 on F4Fs |
| Lt Robert C Coats | VF-17/-18 | 9.333 | 5 on 18/3/45 |
| Lt(jg) Eugene D Redmond | VF-2/-10 | 9.25 | |
| Lt Cdr Paul D Buie | VF-16 | 9 | |
| Lt(jg) Robert B Carlson | VF-30/-40 | 9 | |
| Cdr William M Collins, Jr | VF-8 | 9 | 5 on 12/10/44 |
| Lt Richard T Eastmond | VF-1 | 9 | |
| Lt(jg) Thomas S Harris | VF-18 | 9 | |
| Lt(jg) Daniel R Rehm, Jr | VF-8/-50 | 9 | |
| Lt Arthur Van Haren, Jr | VF-2 | 9 | |
| Lt(jg) Charles E Watts | VF-17/-18 | 8.75 | |
| Lt Robert H Anderson | VF-80 | 8.5 | 5 on 14/12/44 |
| Lt(jg) John L Banks | VF-2 | 8.5 | |
| Ens Carl C Foster | VF-30 | 8.5 | 6 on 6/4/45 |
| Lt(jg) Everett C Hargreaves | VF-2 | 8.5 | 5 on 24/6/44 |
| Ens George W Pigman, Jr | VF-15 | 8.5 | |
| Ens Claude W Plant, Jr | VF-15 | 8.5 | |
| Lt(jg) Luther D Prater, Jr | VF-19 | 8.5 | |
| Ens Larry Self | VF-15 | 8.5 | |
| Lt(jg) Eric A Evenson | VF-30 | 8.25 | |
| Lt John F Gray | VF-5 | 8.25 | |

## 1

**F6F-3 white 00/BuNo 04872 of Cdr James H Flatley, CVAG-5, USS *Yorktown*, 6 May 1943**

Widely respected as one of the Navy's outstanding combat leaders, 'Jimmy' Flatley flew this early-production F6F-3 while commanding Air Group 5 during carrier work-ups in mid-1943. Indeed, BuNo 04872 was the first ever aircraft to land aboard the second *Yorktown*, a feat it accomplished on the above-mentioned date. Note the contemporary roundels and Blue Grey (FS 36118) over Light Grey (FS 36440) scheme, and the '00' 'Double Nuts' modex, now recognised the world over as denoting the CAG's aircraft. The origin of this marking is a little vague, as most CAGs used the modex '99' to decorate their aircraft, with '00' then being used in Navy terminology to denote the admiral. Indeed, Flatley used the callsign '99 Sniper' when airborne, so as not to offend his ranking superiors who may be listening in.

## 2

**F6F-3 white 00 of Cdr James H Flatley, CVAG-5, USS *Yorktown*, 31 August 1943**

This 'Dash Three' was used by Flatley on the Marcus Island raid, and was the second Hellcat to be assigned to the CAG. Like its predecessor it wears his trademark '00' code and an LSO (Landing Signal Officer) stripe on its fin. The Hellcats greatly differ in camouflage schemes, however, this aircraft having been painted in the field in the interim tri-colour scheme of Sea Blue non-specular (FS 35042) over Intermediate Blue (FS 35189), with Insignia White non-specular (FS 37875) undersurfaces. The aircraft's red-bordered fuselage national insignia is smaller than regulations stipulated probably because VF-5 was one of the first F6F squadrons formed, and had to repaint its aircraft from the original factory-applied sea grey/light grey pattern of 1942-43. This machine was later photographed with the red roundel surround crudely painted over, as officially ordered on 31 July 1943.

## 3

**F6F-3 white 37/BuNo 08926 of Lt(jg) Eugene R Hanks, VF-16, USS *Lexington*, 23 November 1943**

Lt(jg) E R Hanks made history in his allotted F6F-3 BuNo 08926 on the morning of 23 November 1943 when he downed three 'Haps' and two Zeros (and possibly a third A6M) in a matter of minutes off Tarawa Island during his combat debut, thus making him the first of 44 Hellcat 'aces in a day'. This aircraft was soon adorned with kill decals upon its recovery back aboard *Lexington*, and Hanks photographed in its cockpit for the newspapers back in America. According to his log book, Hanks never flew BuNo 08926 again after his five-kill mission.

## 4

**F6F-3 white 13/BuNo 66064 of Ens Ed 'Wendy' Wendorf, VF-16, USS *Lexington*, 4 December 1943**

This was the aircraft that Ed Wendorf (4.5 kills) crash-landed back aboard 'Lady Lex' on this date following a frantic action over Kwajalein Atoll. It has often been wrongly described in other volumes as having a red surround to the national insignia, but research for this book has shown that the light shade around the 'star and bar' is in fact blue paint used to touch out the long-since banned red.

## 5

**F6F-3 white 13 *MY OWN JOAN II*/BuNo 25813 of Lt C K 'Ken' Hildebrandt, VF-33, Ondonga, Christmas Day 1943**

All five of Hildebrandt's victories were scored in this machine, which he flew on virtually every sortie during his squadron's spell in the Solomons between August 1943 and January 1944. The early-build F6F-3 bears the VF-33 'Hellcats' insignia forward of the windscreen, along with its nickname and pilot's scoreboard. Like most land-based Hellcats in the Solomons, it has also had its aerial mast removed.

## 6

**F6F-3 white 22 of Lt(jg) Robert W Duncan, VF-5, USS *Yorktown*, late February 1944**

Bob Duncan was the first carrier-based Hellcat pilot to shoot down a Zero, destroying two A6M5s over Wake Island during a fast carrier strike on 5 October 1943, followed by four more Zekes over Truk Atoll on 17 February 1944. He added another Zeke on the 22nd for a total of seven confirmed victories. Duncan was one of seven aces in the squadron led by Lt Cdr Edward M Owen, who contributed five of the unit's 126.5 credited victories. Like *Enterprise*'s VF-10, 'Fighting Five' returned to combat equipped with Corsairs in the final months of the war, flying briefly from *Franklin* in February and March 1945 before the ship was severely damaged in action.

## 7

**F6F-3 white 67/BuNo 40381 of Lt Richard 'Rod' Devine, VF-10, USS *Enterprise*, 17 February 1944**

'Rod' Devine used this 'plain Jane' early-build (note sloping aerial mast) F6F-3 to down a 'Sally' bomber over Truk Lagoon on this date VF-10 bagged 30 aircraft on the 17th, although Devine was the only one to down a 'Sally'. By the time the 'Grim Reapers'' tour had finished in June 1944, 'Rod' Devine had scored eight kills, and finished as the ranking ace of the deployment.

## 8

**F6F-3 white 82/BuNo 26183 of Lt(jg) Donald 'Flash' Gordon, VF-10, USS *Enterprise*, 17 February 1944**

Like Devine, 'Flash' Gordon also got on the scoreboard on the morning of the 17th over Truk, splashing a Zeke (just one of 20) in the one-sided clash. He finished the deployment an ace with five kills, two of which had been scored on VF-10's previous Pacific tour aboard *Enterprise* in F4F-4s in 1942/43.

## 9

**F6F-3 white 19/BuNo 40467 of Lt(jg) Alexander Vraciu, VF-6, USS *Intrepid*, 17 February 1944**

In December 1943 this aircraft was assigned to Alex Vraciu, who shot down seven aircraft with it – four on this date over Truk (three Zekes and a 'Rufe'). The Hellcat sported the regulation squadron markings in addition to personal emblems. Below the canopy rail was stencilled *VRACIU*, while VF-6's 'Felix the Cat' emblem shared space with a personal insignia of unknown origin – a red-faced bull's head on a yellow background. The nickname *Gadget* was rendered in white script, presumably applied by the plane captain or other maintenance personnel. The fuselage of this very aeroplane somehow survived the wholesale scrapping of Hellcats after the war, and has been married to the wings and tail of F6F-5K BuNo 80141 and restored to airworthy

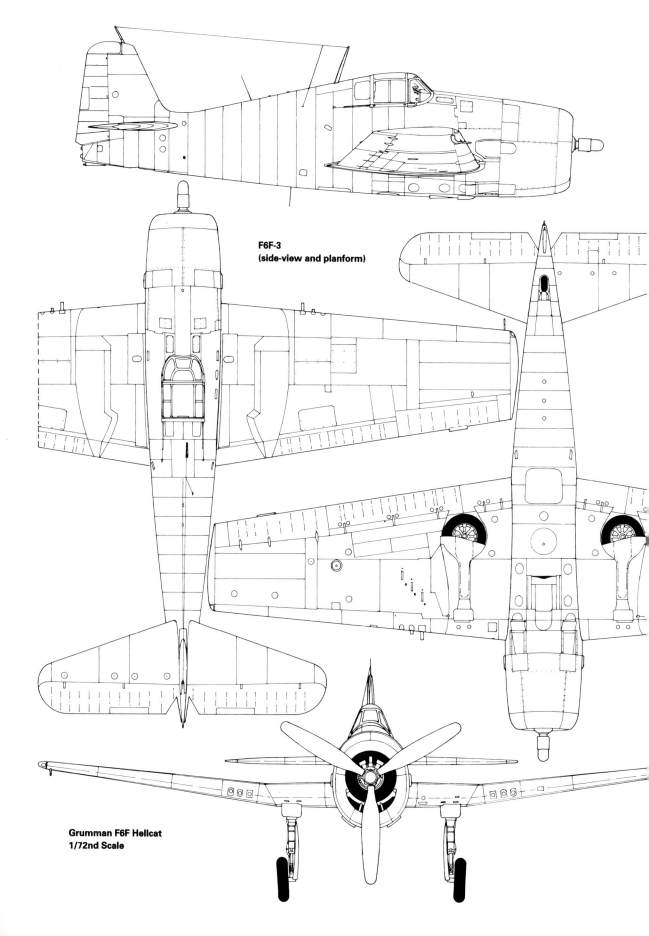

F6F-3
(side-view and planform)

Grumman F6F Hellcat
1/72nd Scale

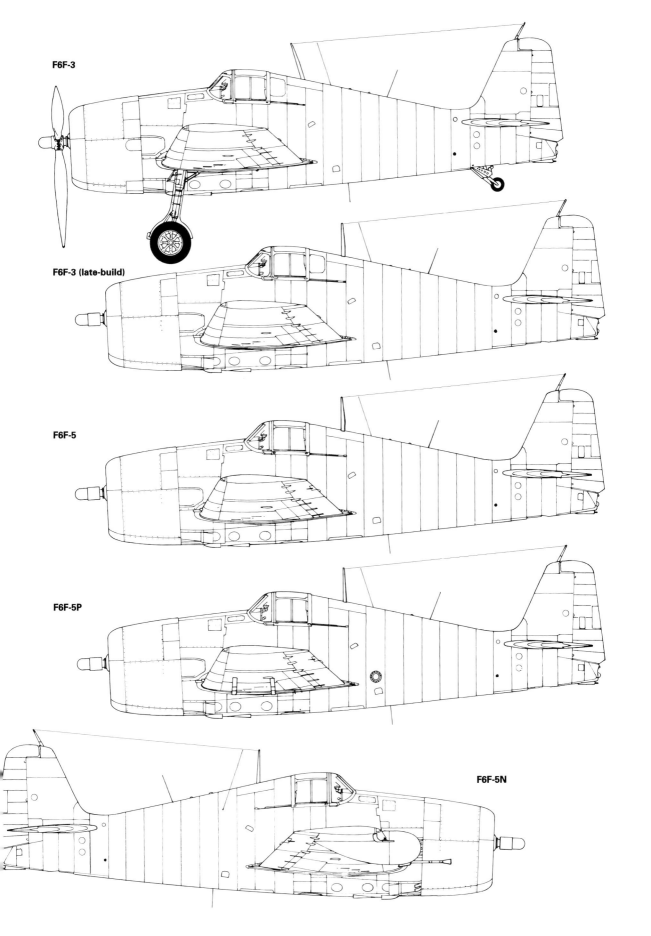

F6F-3

F6F-3 (late-build)

F6F-5

F6F-5P

F6F-5N

condition. It is presently owned and flown by The Fighter Collection at Duxford, in England.

## 10

### F6F-3 white 33 of Lt(jg) Frank Fleming, VF-16, USS *Lexington*, April 1944

Frank Fleming was among the earliest Hellcat pilots to gain confirmed victories against Japanese aircraft. By the end of 1943 he had been credited with 4.5 victories, and went on to complete his tour aboard *Lexington* with 7.5. Although personally-assigned aircraft were seldom flown by their designated pilot, some squadrons such as VF-16 made the effort. Aside from Fleming's kill decals, 'white 33' also wears a 'Fighting Airedale' insignia forward of the windscreen.

## 11

### Hellcat I JV125 of Lt Cdr Stanley G Orr, No 804 Sqn, HMS *Emperor*, 14 May 1944

This drably-marked Hellcat I was used by Lt Cdr Orr to attack a formation of He 115 floatplanes off the coast of Norway on this date. Delivered to No 804 Sqn as an attrition replacement in early May following the unit's return from the April *Tirpitz* raids, JV125's service records are a little vague after its initial successes off Norway. Its only other entries of note whilst in FAA service were that it was delivered to Shorts of Belfast for repair following a Cat B accident in early 1945, and that it did not return to airworthiness until 22 December that year.

## 12

### F6F-3 white 5/BuNo 40315 of Lt Hollis 'Holly' Hills , VF-32, USS *Langley*, 30 April 1944

Having already earned a place in the history books by scoring the first ever kill in a Mustang (see *Aces 7 Mustang Aces of the Ninth and Fifteenth Air Forces and the RAF*), Hollis Hills became a naval aviator in late 1942, and helped form VF-32. He considered himself to be a good shot, and had a chance to show his ability when his new unit went into combat in 1944. Employing German 'Yo-Yo' tactics of diving into a target, making one firing pass and then using his speed to quickly regain altitude, Hills used this aircraft, callsign 'Steele 5', to down three Zekes over Truk Atoll on 29 April.

## 13

### F6F-3 white 31/BuNo 69532 of Wilbur B 'Spider' Webb, VF-2, USS *Hornet*, 19 June 1944

Webb flew 'White 31' over Guam during a single-handed interception of Japanese aircraft in the Orote Field traffic pattern on this date. In a few minutes he had shot down six Aichi D3A 'Vals' confirmed and two probables, becoming one of six Hellcat 'aces in a day' during the 'Great Marianas Turkey Shoot' – all this despite having persistent gun failure due to a lack of hydraulic pressure in the weapons' charger system. Webb landed back aboard ship with a barely functioning undercarriage, no canopy and minus his flying helmet, which had been shot off – he was unhurt, however. In all, 147 bullet and shrapnel holes were found in BuNo 69532, and after parts reclamation, it was honourably 'buried at sea'.

## 14

### F6F-3 *The Minsi* of Cdr David McCampbell, Commander Air Group 15, USS *Essex*, 19 June 1944

*The Minsi* was the second Hellcat assigned to the Navy's leading fighter ace, Cdr David McCampbell. His first F6F-3 was BuNo 41692, nicknamed *Monsoon Maiden*, which he flew during his time as CO of VF-15, and which was jettisoned from *Essex* on 20 May 1944 due irreparable flak

damage the day before over Marcus Island. This machine was issued to him as a replacement, and he named for his lady friend, *Miss Mary Blatz*. It too was stricken with flak damage over Manila in September 1944, and duly replaced by F6F-5 *Minsi II*. McCampbell flew *The Minsi* on at least one of his two sorties of 19 June, accounting for five 'Judys' in the first and two Zekes in the second. The horizontal band around the vertical stabiliser and rudder was an *Essex* trademark which remained when CVG-4 relieved CVG-15 in November. None of McCampbell's 'CAG birds' had side number.

## 15

### F6F-3 white 36/BuNo 41269 of Ens Wilbur B 'Spider' Webb, VF-2, USS *Hornet*, 20 June 1944

This was one of four machines used by Webb during the Marianas campaign, 'White 36' being flown by the newly-crowned ace on the 'Flight after Darkness' assault on the retreating Japanese fleet staged 24 hours after his epic Guam sortie. TF-38 launched 216 aircraft to strike the shattered enemy at extreme range, knowing that the force would have to recover back aboard in darkness – few pilots were night landing-qualified in 1944. Webb returned safely in BuNo 41269, but 104 aircraft were lost.

## 16

### F6F-3 white 32 of Lt(jg) Alexander Vraciu, VF-16, USS *Lexington*, 21 June 1944

Following the torpedoing of *Intrepid* at Truk on 17 February, VF-6 was sent back the US, but Alex Vraciu somehow managed to wangle a transfer to VF-16, and thus remain in combat until the middle of the year. He had been the leading ace in his previous unit, and went on to top VF-16's list of high scorers also. Vraciu was assigned aircraft number 32 (BuNo unknown) whilst with his new unit, which carried his name and ultimate tally of 19 victories. It is uncertain whether he flew this Hellcat during his interception of Japanese dive-bombers over TF-58 on 19 June, which resulted in six kills in only eight minutes. One source indicates that he flew number 13 on that occasion, but the origin of that statement is unknown.

## 17

### F6F-3 white 9/BuNo 40090 of Lt William C Moseley, VF-1, USS *Yorktown*, June 1944

This machine was issued to five-kill ace Moseley in late June as a replacement for BuNo 41438, which had had to be jettisoned over the side of *Yorktown* following aerial combat (in which he downed two Zekes and claimed a third as a probable) on the 19th of that month near Guam. This machine still wears its crudely-applied ferry code (the last three numbers of its BuNo) on its cowling.

## 18

### F6F-3N white 9/BuNo 42158 of Lt Russ Reiserer, VF(N)-76 Det 2, USS *Hornet*, 10 July 1944

This rare F6F-3N was used by Reiserer when he flew to Saipan on this date to discuss operating procedures with a USAAF P-61 Black Widow unit that was patrolling the same night skies. Three days earlier he had used similarly-marked BuNo 26077 to down his ninth, and last, kill (a 'Betty') on a night CAP that lasted almost four hours. This was Reiserer's sole nocturnal score. Note the mixed scheme on this fighter, its matt blue tail contrasting sharply with its overall glossy sea blue fuselage and wings.

## 19

### F6F-5 white 8 of Ensigns Alfred R Wood and Edward W

**Olszewski, VOF-1, USS *Tulagi*, August 1944**

Incredibly, of the six Luftwaffe aircraft claimed by the gunnery-spotting VOF-1 during Operation *Dragoon*, this Hellcat was involved in the destruction of four of them – Ens Wood shared in the destruction of two He 111s near Vienne on 19 August, and Ens Olszewski downed a pair of Ju 52s near Orange two days later. Both pilots went on to score kills in the Pacific with the redesignated VOC-1 in 1945.

**20**

**F6F-5 white 12/BuNo 58937 of Lt(jg) Ray 'Hawk' Hawkins, VF-31, USS *Cabot*, September 1944**

Texan 'Hawk' Hawkins was the second-ranking ace of VF-31 'Flying Meataxes' with 14 kills, five ('Oscars') of which were scored on 13 September 1944. Assigned a mixed fleet of 14 'Dash Threes' and 10 'Dash Fives', the unit produced 14 aces during its 1944 deployment. Its overall wartime tally of 165.5 aircraft made it the top-scoring CVL fighter squadron in the Navy.

**21**

**F6F-5N white 13/BuNo 70147 of Lt Bill Henry Hawkins, VF(N)-41, USS *Independence*, 21 September 1944**

The first dedicated night air group in the US Navy, CVLG(N)-41 deployed in the light carrier *Independence* in August 1944. The fighter squadron under Lt Cdr T F Caldwell shot down 46 Japanese aircraft, producing two aces, Exec Lt W E Henry with 9.5 victories and Ens J A Berkheimer, who was killed with his score standing at seven. Relatively few of the aerial victories were achieved in darkness, however, owing to slow acceptance of the night fliers' capabilities by TF-58. A perfect example of this occurred on 21 September when Henry used BuNo 70147, callsign 'Cupid 13', to score a probable 'Oscar' kill over Clark Field at 9.35 am!

**22**

**F6F-3 white 3 of Ens Gordon A Stanley, VF-27, USS *Princeton*, September 1944**

Like most of 'Fighting 27's' distinctively-marked Hellcats, this machine went to the bottom of the Pacific with *Princeton* on 24 October 1944 following the carrier's mortal wounding by a well-placed bomb dropped from a lone 'Judy'. It was the regular mount of eight-kill ace Gordon Stanley, who had the distinction of scoring all his victories in pairs! Stanley was to later die in an F9F-6 crash in 1956.

**23**

**F6F-3 white 17 of Lt Richard Stambook, VF-27, USS *Princeton*, 24 October 1944**

Stambook was VF-27's third-highest scorer on their 1944 deployment, having claimed his final kill (a 'Nick') six days prior to *Princeton*'s sinking. A seasoned pilot by the time he saw combat with VF-27 in 1944, 'Dick' Stambook had earlier served with VS-3 on Dauntlesses and VF-6 and VF-3 on Wildcats.

**24**

**F6F-3 white 13 of Lt William E Lamb, VF-27, USS *Princeton*, 24 October 1944**

A pre-war naval aviator, William Lamb served as VF-27's Exec from June 1944. This promotion seemed to inspire Lamb greatly for he proceeded to 'make ace' in the space of ten days between the 19th and 29th of that month. He went on to add a sixth kill to his World War 2 record on 18 November 1950 when he shot down a MiG-15 over North Korea whilst serving as CO of F9F-3 Panther-equipped VF-52 aboard USS *Valley Forge* (see *Aces 4 Korean War Aces*).

**25**

**F6F-3 white 23 of Lt James 'Red' Shirley, VF-27, USS *Princeton*, 24 October 1944**

This was the aircraft used by ranking VF-27 ace Shirley to down five fighters in a frenetic dogfight that occurred west of the task force on this date. The Hellcat was destined never to carry his final scoreboard of 12.5 kills as it was lost with *Princeton* later that day. Rated as an exceptional pilot, Shirley had been 'ploughed back' into the Navy's training programme at Pensacola as an instructor upon earning his wings in early 1942, and had had to fight to get a frontline posting late the following year.

**26**

**F6F-5 white 9 of Lt Carl A Brown, Jr, VF-27, USS *Princeton*, 24 October 1944**

Although assigned to VF-27's second-highest scorer, this particular Hellcat was not being flown by him on this date. Indeed, with the loss of all squadron records (and pilots' log books) on the 24th, it cannot be ascertained if this aircraft was used by him to down any of the 5.5 kills it is marked up with. This near-new Hellcat was one of six F6F-5 replacements issued to the squadron prior to the Leyte Gulf campaign, operating side-by-side with the far more common tri-colour 'Dash Threes'.

**27**

**F6F-5 white 10 *PAOLI LOCAL* of Ens Paul E Drury, VF-27, USS *Princeton*, 24 October 1944**

Like Carl Brown's Hellcat, this machine was not flown by its regular pilot, 6.5-kill ace Paul Drury, on 24 October. Such was the hurry to scramble VF-27's fighters, pilots strapped into whatever aircraft they could find serviceable – not that an unfamiliar cockpit put Drury off for he downed three fighters in the bloody clash. Named after a Philadelphia commuter train that he used to catch near his home, Drury's *PAOLI LOCAL* was flown into combat on this fateful day by recently-arrived replacement pilot Ens O L Scott, who was subsequently shot down and killed – VF-27's only aerial loss on this day.

**28**

**F6F-5 white 1 of Lt Cdr Fred A Bardshar, CO of VF-27/Commander Air Group 27, USS *Princeton*, 24 October 1944**

The pilot of this Hellcat held the distinction of commanding both VF-27 and Air Group 27 for much of *Princeton*'s combat deployment. Previously the unit's Exec, Fred Bardshar proved more than up to the job(s) thrust upon him following the death in combat of the previous incumbent, Cdr E W Wood, on 19 June 1944 – the same day the former splashed two 'Judys'. Bardshar's final score of 7.5 kills was marked in the usual fashion on the starboard side of the fuselage on this machine.

**29**

**F6F-5 white 7 *PAPER DOLL* of Ens Bob Burnell, VF-27, USS *Princeton*, 24 October 1944**

Although bearing Burnell's name, scoreboard (four kills in total) and personal marking, this F6F-5 was flown by Carl Brown, Jr, on the 24th, the latter using it to down five Zekes before landing back aboard *Essex*. Both pilot and aircraft were badly shot up in this combat, but by recovering back aboard ship rather than ditching, PAPER DOLL became one of just nine (out of 24) VF-27 Hellcats to survive the sinking of *Princeton*. Prior to the unit deploying aboard ship, Burnell had hand-painted the cat's teeth on all 24 F6Fs assigned to VF-27.

## 30

**F6F-5 *Minsi III*/BuNo 70143 of Cdr David McCampbell, Commander Air Group 15, USS *Essex*, 25 October 1944**
Easily the best-known Hellcat of them all, BuNo 70143 was an early production F6F-5 that retained the 'windows' behind the cockpit as per the F6F-3 – a feature deleted on most 'Dash Fives'. As an air group commander, McCampbell was able to fly his assigned aircraft on nearly every mission, and *Minsi III* lasted far longer than either of his previous *Minsi*s. Although McCampbell lost his logbooks after the war, it is estimated that he scored 20 or more of his 34 confirmed victories in *Minsi III*. Sadly, this machine was lost in an accident in December 1944 whilst being flown by McCampbell's replacement.

## 31

**F6F-5 white 28/BuNo 58069 of Ens Frank 'Trooper' Troup, VF-29, USS *Cabot*, 29 October 1944**
VF-29 replaced the battle-weary VF-31 aboard *Cabot* on 5 October 1944, and immediately adorned their F6F-5s in identical markings – 'G symbols' tended to be associated more with the carrier than the air group. Frank Troup used this aircraft to down a 'Jack' and a 'Tojo' over Clark Field during an early-morning sweep on this date. However, his aircraft was badly shot up by a second 'Jack' soon after he had despatched the 'Tojo', and Troup was forced to ditch the fighter during his return – he was soon rescued by the destroyer USS *Halsey Powell*, however. Frank Troup finished the war with seven kills.

## 32

**F6F-5 *Minsi II* of Cdr David McCampbell, Commander Air Group 15, USS *Essex*, October 1944**
This aircraft was one of the first F6F-5s issued to Air Group 15, and naturally was assigned to the ranking pilot aboard *Essex*. It was flown very infrequently when compared with McCampbell's previous Hellcats, as its pilot was not fond of its engine unreliability – it suffered two powerplant failures in very short order whilst the CAG was airborne in it, and following air combat damage, was renamed and passed on to a line pilot from VF-15.

## 33

**F6F-5 white 29 of Lt James S Swope, VF-11, USS *Hornet*, October 1944**
Devoid of any distinguishing markings other than the white ball 'G symbol' on the tail and a similarly-coloured propeller hub, this Hellcat was occassionally flown by combat veteran Jim Swope during the latter half of VF-11's frontline deployment on *Hornet*. A pre-war private pilot, Swope had joined the 'Sundowners' as early as September 1942 – just in time to deploy to Guadalcanal, where he claimed 4.666 kills in Wildcats. He followed up this success with a further five kills scored whilst leading his four-Hellcat division, which included six-kill ace Lt(jg) Blake Moranville as section leader.

## 34

**F6F-5 white 25 of Lt Bruce Williams, VF-19, USS *Lexington*, October 1944**
This early-build F6F-5 was one of just a handful to serve in the frontline in the old tricolour scheme of 1943. Aside from its odd shading, the fighter also boasts its modex repeated immediately aft of the cockpit – a marking unique to VF-19, and one which was decidedly non-regulation. Seven-kill ace 'Willie Mohawk' Williams was responsible for bringing one of the most gravely damaged Hellcats safely back aboard ship when he recovered in F6F-3 BuNo 42054 on 21 October

1944. He had been strafing ammunition barges off Ceram, in the Philippines, at low-level when one exploded just below his fighter. The Hellcat was 'tossed' from 50 to 150 ft as a result of the blast, freezing all the cockpit instruments and leaving Williams upside down with his right wing in shreds. Somehow he got back aboard *Lexington*, where a survey of the damage revealed twisted structural spars in the right wing, a warped tail surface, cancelling his aileron control, and a foot-long chunk of 'two-by-four' wooden plank lodged in the engine.

## 35

**F6F-5 white 71 of Lt Leo B McCuddin, VF-20, USS *Enterprise*, October 1944**
'Fighting Squadron 20' embarked in *Enterprise* in August 1944, logging combat missions over the Philippines and Formosa. Among the nine aces were Lt(jg) Douglas Baker with 16.333 victories and the CO, Cdr Fred Bakutis, with 11. The pilot of this Hellcat, Lt McCudden scored five victories over Japanese fighters in three combats, all in the space of six days. Although he flew 'White 71' at least once in combat, the six victory flags below its cockpit probably represent the aircraft's tally, rather than any single pilot. After transferring to *Lexington* in December, VF-20 completed its tour in January 1945 with 158 kills.

## 36

**F6F-5 white 13/BuNo 42013 of Lt(jg) Ed Copeland, VF-19, USS *Lexington*, 6 November 1944**
Unlucky for some, 'white 13' was ditched in Luguna do Bay by six-kill ace Ed Copeland after it had sustained AA damage over Manila on this date. Fortunately, he was soon rescued by Filipino guerillas, who hid him until he could be picked up by a PBY. All of Copeland's kills, and his sole probable, were scored against different types of aircraft, which must some kind of Navy record.

## 37

**F6F-5 white 99 of Cdr T Hugh Winters, Jr, Commander Air Group 19, USS *Lexington*, November 1944**
The original skipper of 'Fighting 19', Cdr Winters became *Lexington*'s air group commander in September 1944. He flew two 'CAG birds', both similarly-marked with 'number 99', and used the radio callsign '99 Mohawk'. The first *Hanger Lily* (a misnomer referring to the ship's hangar deck) was damaged by flak and jettisoned. The second eventually sported eight victory decals, plus the name and an appropriate flower painted forward of the windscreen – 'COMDR T H WINTERS' was stencilled below the cockpit as well. Owing to the loss of his logbooks, neither BuNo is known.

## 38

**F6F-5 white 9 of Lt Charles 'Skull' Stimpson, VF-11, USS *Hornet*, November 1944**
VF-11's leading ace on both of its frontline deployments, Charlie Stimpson scored his first six victories flying F4F-4s at Guadalcanal in 1943. A further ten kills (all fighters) were accrued by 'Skull' in four-week scoring spree in October/November 1944, thus giving him a wartime total of 16. This aircraft was specially adorned with the appropriate number of kill decals for photographic purposes only.

## 39

**F6F-5 white 30/BuNo 70680 of Lt(jg) Blake Moranville, VF-11, USS *Hornet*, January 1945**
The callsign of this F6F was 'Ginger 30', reflecting its base as

*Hornet*. Six-kill ace Moranville was shot down by a single well-aimed 20 mm AA round whilst strafing ground targets in this aeroplane near Saigon, Indochina, on 12 January 1945. Captured by the Vichy French, Moranville, and several other downed fliers, experienced an odyssey which took them from Saigon to Hanoi, on to Dien Bien Phu and then into China, and safety.

## 40

**F6F-5 white 9 of Lt Hamilton McWhorter, III, VF-12, USS *Randolph*, January 1945**

'Ham' McWhorter was not only the first Hellcat ace but also the first double ace as well, flying with VF-9 aboard *Essex* in 1943-44. He scored his first victory at Wake Island on 5 October 1943, his fifth in the Gilberts on 19 November and tenth at Truk Atoll on 17 February 1944. Many 'Fighting Nine' pilots later joined Air Group 12, including Armistead B Smith, Reuben Denoff, John M Franks and Harold Vita, who all became aces. McWhorter scored his 11th success a year after the Truk raid, downing a Zeke near Tokyo on 16 February 1945. He added a 'Myrt' reconnaissance aircraft on 13 May for a wartime total of 12. Aside from the distinctive white stripes on the vertical stabiliser, Air Group 12 aircraft also had white ailerons.

## 41

**F6F-5 white 74/BuNo 72354 of Lt John M Wesolowski, VBF-9, USS *Yorktown*, 11 April 1945**

Already a five-kill Wildcat ace following his tour with VF-5 on Guadalcanal in late 1942, Wesolowski then served as a flight instructor for almost two years, before being posted in January 1945 to the newly-created VBF-9 as Exec. He scored two kills over Okinawa during his second frontline tour, the first of which was against the ultimate Japanese naval fighter, the Kawanishi N1K2-J *Shiden-Kai* 'George'. Claimed on 11 April in this Hellcat, Wesolowski's 'George' was the only one of its type downed by *Yorktown*'s air group.

## 42

**F6F-5 white 2 of Lt Cdr Robert A Weatherup, VF-46, USS *Independence*, 15 April 1945**

Four days after Wesolowski bagged a 'George', VF-46's Exec, Lt Cdr 'Doc' Weatherup, went one better by downing a pair of *Shiden-Kai* over Kanoya Airfield, on Kyushu – his only wartime kills. One of the fighters was flown by Navy ace Shoichi Sugita (between 30 and 70 kills), and his wingman Toyomi Miyazawa was in the second 'George'. Both part of the elite 343rd *Kokutai* which included Saburo Sakai amongst its ranks (he actually witnessed the attack from the ground), the two Japanese pilots were caught whilst attempting to take-off following a rocket and strafing attack by VF-46.

## 43

**F6F-5 white 7 of Ens Robert E Murray, VF-29, USS *Cabot*, April 1945**

Lt(jg) R E Murray was VF-29's 'topgun' with 10.33 confirmed kills, the unit producing a further 11 aces. Operating against Japan, VF-29 claimed 113 victories, including 34 off Formosa on 16 October 1944 – Murray claimed four on this day to achieve ace status. Aside from carrying 12 flags, denoting that both Murray's shared 'Betty' claim and a damaged Zeke had also been included in the tally, 15 bombing mission symbols have been painstakingly added to the fuselage of 'Lucky 7'.

## 44

**F6F-5 white 115 *DEATH N' DESTRUCTION*/BuNo 72534 of Ensigns Donald McPherson, Bill Kingston, Jr, and Lyttleton Ward, VF-83, USS *Essex*, 5 May 1945**

Carrying gaudy nose-art and a victory tally of nine kills, BuNo 72534 was arguably the most recognisable Hellcat aboard *Essex* in the last months of the war. Predominantly flown by a trio of ensign aces, the fighter's greatest day came on 4 May 1945 when it was used by Lyttleton Ward to down three 'Alfs' and an 'Oscar' as VF-83 helped repel one of the biggest *kamikaze* raids launched on TF-58 during the Okinawan invasion.

## 45

**F6F-5N white F(N)76/BuNo 78669 of Maj Robert B Porter, VMF(N)-542, Okinawa, 15 June 1945**

Bruce Porter logged three victories while flying F4Us with VMF-121 in the Solomons during 1943. He became an ace on the night of 15 June 1945 when he shot down a 'Nick' and a 'Betty' mothership, complete with *Ohka* suicide bomb, off the coast of Okinawa. Upon assuming command of VMF(N)-542 some weeks earlier, Porter had inherited the previous CO's (Maj W C Kellum) 'F(N)76', which was the only Hellcat in the squadron fitted with cannon armament. It was then adorned with the name *Millie Lou*, but the new CO insisted upon a more warlike appellation, and chose *Black Death*. He also had a bottle of Schenley's whiskey painted on the starboard cowling. 'F(N)76' was also stencilled in white on each landing-gear door, and Porter's victories were displayed on the left side of the fuselage below the cockpit.

## 46

**F6F-5N black F(N)4/BuNo 78704 of Capt Robert Baird, VMF(N)-533, Okinawa, June 1945**

The Marine Corps' only nightfighter ace, Baird had previously flown F4U-2s with VMF(N)-532 in the Central Pacific, but had enjoyed little success with the Chance-Vought machine. He arrived on Okinawa with VMF(N)-533 in April 1945, and became an ace over a two-week period in June. He claimed his first victory, a 'Jake' floatplane, on 9 June, followed by two 'doubles' – a 'Betty' and a 'Nell' on the 16th, then a 'Fran' and 'Betty' six nights later. His sixth, and final, victim, another 'Betty', was splashed on 14 July. Like many nightfighter pilots, he preferred cannons, but only scored his last victory with the 20 mm weapons owing to previous functioning problems.

## 47

**F6F-5 white VS 1 of Lt Cdr Willard E Eder, 'Victory Squadron', late 1945**

At the end of World War 2 the Navy and Treasury Departments combined in a final bond drive to defray demobilisation costs. The 'Victory Squadron' was established under Lt Cdr Eder, who had led Air Group 29 in 1944-45. His personal Hellcat included a detailed score board depicting his seven aerial victories (one shared), plus three Vichy and nine Japanese aircraft destroyed on the ground, in addition to 39 bombing sorties. Other aircraft in the squadron were F7Fs, F4Us, SB2Cs, TBMs and two captured Japanese aircraft – a Zeke and a 'Kate'. Another ace in the unit was Capt 'Gus' Thomas, a Marine Corps Corsair ace who scored 18.5 kills during two tours with VMF-213.

# FIGURE PLATES

## 1

Lt Cdr Paul D Buie, CO of VF-16, has unfolded his mission map and is explaining to his pilots up on the deck of *Lexington* where the next sweep will take place over Tarawa on the morning of 23 November 1943. He is wearing an AN-H-15 tropical issue flying helmet, customised in squadron colours by the unit's groundcrew. Other pilots in VF-15 had their head gear embellished with a green shamrock hand-painted on top of the cloth helmet. Buie's goggles are standard military-issue Polaroid B-8s, which had only been cleared for frontline use the previous month. As commanding officer, he has chosen to wear a khaki shirt and trousers, rather than the more common 'suit/summer/flying', and complements this smarter apparel with a pair of highly-polished black lace-up shoes.

## 2

Looking a little more 'combat-wise' in his well-worn flying 'coveralls' than the 'spotless' Buie, Lt(jg) Alex Vraciu displays his final score after his epic struggle against a formation of 'Judys' on 19 June 1944. His headwear consists of a later spec AN-H-15 helmet combined with an old pair of favourite AN-6530, or B-7, goggles. Like Buie, Vraciu's life preserver is a ubiquitous N2885. He is still wearing his dinghy pack, having just jumped out of his Hellcat, and his hands are adorned in fire-proof naval aviator's gloves. Finally, Vraciu is wearing standard QMC-issue 'Boondockers' on his feet.

## 3

Wearing fundamentally similar clothing as Vraciu, Lt Jim Swope of VF-11 in January 1945 also has his seat-type parachute strapped on his back below the dinghy pack. His helmet is similar in design to Buie's, but his goggles are B-7s. Most pilots chose to carry just a Smith and Wesson .38 revolver when going into combat, but Swope has also opted for the added protection of a jungle knife, secured in its leather scabbard.

## 4

Lt Cdr Stanley Orr, CO of No 804 Sqn on HMS *Emperor* in April 1944, checks over the charts prior to launching against *Tirpitz*. Although wearing a standard Royal Navy dark blue flying overall, adorned with 'two-and-a-half' rank tabs, and fully tied-up Mae West, Orr's head gear is American in origin – a modified AN-H-15, complete with B-7 goggles. He had acquired these whilst in Norfolk, Virginia, working up with the newly-formed No 896 Sqn on Martlet IVs in October 1942. His oxygen mask is RAF issue, however. In order to stave off the cold should he have to ditch in fjord, Orr is also wearing a turtle neck woollen sweater underneath his overall. The webbing belt for his .38 service revolver is attach to the bottom of his Mae West.

## 5

As befits the senior pilot aboard ship, CAG-15 Cdr David McCampbell is wearing a khaki button-up shirt and matching trousers similar in style to Lt Cdr P D Buie's. His equipment is all standard Navy issue, and he has a Smith and Wesson .38 revolver holstered beneath his left arm, with a bandoleer well-stocked with ammunition slung over his right shoulder beneath the life preserver. McCampbell has also chosen the later B-8 goggles in preference to the older B-7s favoured by a number of seasoned combat veterans.

## 6

Maj Bruce Porter, CO of VMF(N)-542, is also wearing as shirt and trousers as befits his rank. Unlike the carrier-based aviators seen on this spread, Porter has chosen not to adorn his N2885 with various dye marker pouches and flare rounds. Note too that he written his name on the crotch strap of the life preserver, thus preventing anyone from 'borrowing' it by mistake! Unlike his pilots, who would be equipped with well-worn 'Boondockers', Porter is wearing a shiny pair of dress brown leather lace ups, which look rather smarter with the shirt and trousers.

# BIBLIOGRAPHY

**Hata, I and Izawa, Y** *Japanese Naval Aces and Fighter Units.* Naval Institute Press, Annapolis, Maryland, 1989

**Olynyk, F** *US Navy Victory Credits for Destruction of Enemy Aircraft in Aerial Combat, World War II.* Privately published, 1982

**Olynyk, F** *Stars & Bars, A Tribute to the American Fighter Ace 1920-73.* Grub Street, London, England, 1995

**Brown, J D** *Carrier Operations in World War II. Vol. I: The Royal Navy.* Ian Allan, London, England, 1968

**Polmar, N** *Aircraft Carriers.* Doubleday, New York, 1969

**Sturtivant, R** *British Naval Aviation: Fleet Air Arm, 1917-1990.* Naval Institute Press, Annapolis, Maryland, 1990

**Sturtivant, R and Ballance, T** *The Squadrons of the Fleet Air Arm,* Air Britain Publications, 1994, Tonbridge, Kent

**Tillman, B** *Carrier Battle in the Philippine Sea.* Phalanx, St Paul, Minnesota, 1994

**Tillman, B** *Hellcat: the F6F in World War II.* Naval Institute Press, Annapolis, Maryland, 1979

**Tillman, B** *Wildcat Aces of World War 2.* Osprey Aerospace Publishing, London, England, 1995

**Styling, M** *Corsair Aces of World War 2.* Osprey Aerospace Publishing, London, England, 1996

**Toliver, R and Constable, T** *Fighter Aces.* Macmillan, New York, 1965

**Winters, T H** *Skipper: Confessions of a Fighter Squadron Commander.* Champlin Fighter Museum Press, Mesa, Arizona, 1985